What Is a
Dirigible?

What Is an
Adam's Apple?

What Is
Zorbing?

WHAT Is
Dyslexia?

What Is
Spelunking?

WHAT Was the
Roanoke Colony?

What Is
Ratha Yatra?

What Is
Skara Brae?

What Is an
Orrery?

WHAT Is
an Aye-Aye?

WHAT Is a
Daguerreotype?

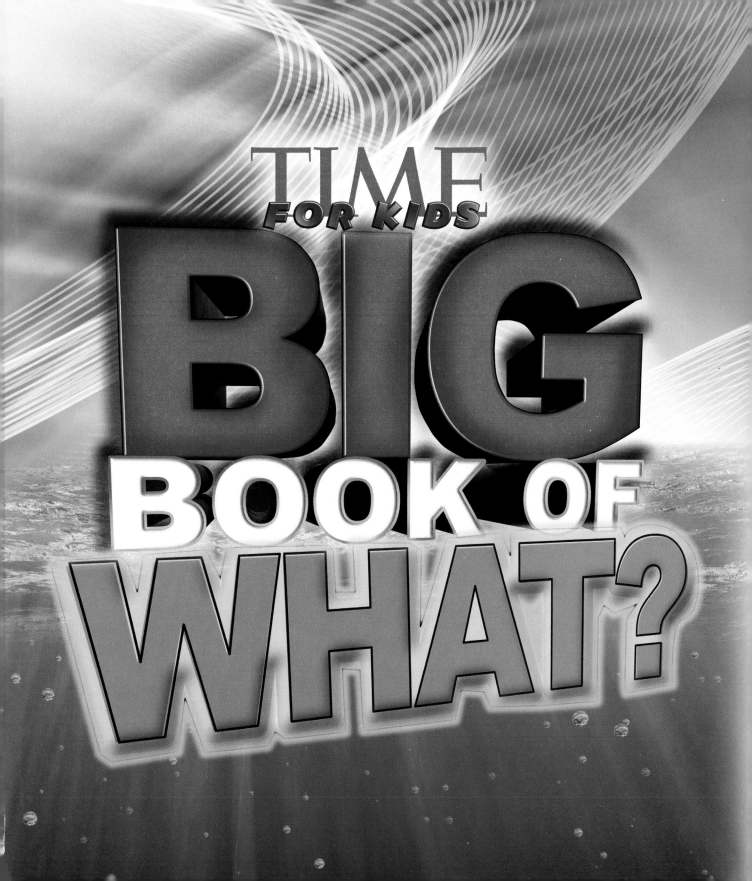

TIME FOR KIDS

Managing Editor, TIME For Kids: Nellie Gonzalez Cutler
Editor, Time Learning Ventures: Jonathan Rosenbloom

Book Packager: R studio T, New York City
Art Direction/Design: Raúl Rodriguez and Rebecca Tachna
Writer: Catherine Nichols
Illustrator: Chris Reed
Photo Researchers: Miriam Budnick, Elizabeth Vezzulla
Designers: Fabian Contreras, Ames Montgomery
Copyeditor: Joe Bomba
Indexer: Charles Karchmer
Fact Checkers: Luis Pereyra, Audrey Whitley

TIME HOME ENTERTAINMENT

Publisher: Richard Fraiman
Vice President, Business Development & Strategy: Steven Sandonato
Executive Director, Marketing Services: Carol Pittard
Executive Director, Retail & Special Sales: Tom Mifsud
Executive Publishing Director: Joy Butts
Director, Bookazine Development & Marketing: Laura Adam
Finance Director: Glenn Buonocore
Assistant General Counsel: Helen Wan
Assistant Director, Special Sales: Ilene Schreider
Senior Book Production Manager: Susan Chodakiewicz
Design & Prepress Manager: Anne-Michelle Gallero
Brand Manager: Jonathan White
Associate Prepress Manager: Alex Voznesenskiy

Editorial Director: Stephen Koepp

Special thanks: Christine Austin, Jeremy Biloon, Jim Childs, Rose Cirrincione, Lauren Hall Clark, Jacqueline Fitzgerald, Christine Font, Jenna Goldberg, Hillary Hirsch, Suzanne Janso, Raphael Joa, Amy Mangus, Robert Marasco, Kimberly Marshall, Amy Migliaccio, Nina Mistry, Dave Rozzelle, Adriana Tierno, Vanessa Wu

For information on TIME For Kids magazine for the classroom or home, go to TIMEFORKIDS.COM or call 1-800-777-8600. For subscriptions to SI KIDS, go to SIKIDS.COM or call 1-800-889-6007.

Published by TIME For Kids Books,
An imprint of Time Home Entertainment Inc.
135 West 50th Street
New York, NY 10020

ISBN 10: 1-60320-241-2
ISBN 13: 978-1-60320-241-1
Library of Congress Control Number: 2012931016

TIME For Kids is a trademark of Time Inc.

We welcome your comments and suggestions about TIME For Kids Books. Please write to us at:
TIME For Kids Books, Attention: Book Editors, P.O. Box 11016, Des Moines, IA 50336-1016
If you would like to order any of our hardcover Collector's Edition books, please call us at 1-800-327-6388 (Monday through Friday, 7 a.m. to 8 p.m., or Saturday, 7 a.m. to 6 p.m., Central Time).

1 QGT 12

Contents

How to Use This Book

This book is filled with answers to many questions asked by kids—and even some grown-ups. What is a dog's most powerful sense? What are some insects you can eat? What does it mean to be double-jointed? The answers to these questions—and many more—are explained clearly on the following pages. The *Big Book of What* contains 12 chapters covering topics from sports and history to animals and inventions. In some chapters, you'll find activities or experiments that are fun to try. And on every page you'll find surprising facts and trivia. Plus: A bonus glossary defines some words you can use to impress your friends!

Explanation: Here's where you'll find detailed answers to the question at the top of the page.

What's More...: Learn more awesome facts and trivia about the subject.

Information Boxes: Short sidebar articles and lists give you more information about the topic.

Try It!: Easy, fun activities and experiments provide hands-on experiences.

WHAT Is a Boomerang?

The boomerang is a curved missile that spins through the air and may return to the thrower. Boomerangs have been around for a very long time. One discovered in Poland, was carved from a mammoth's tusk and is about 30,000 years old. Experts say it was a non-returning boomerang—it didn't come back after it was thrown. They think it was used as a weapon to hunt animals.

Returning boomerangs were first used in Australia about 10,000 years ago. There, the native people, called Aborigines, developed a returning boomerang for fun and sport. And that's the role they still play today.

Modern boomerangs can be shaped like a banana, an *X*, or a question mark. Today's versions are made from a variety of materials, including plywood, plastic, aluminum, and fiberglass.

WHAT's More...

Boomerang fans test their skills at tournaments. They compete at different events, such as long distance, doubling (throwing two boomerangs at the same time), and fast catch (the most catches in five minutes).

A player competes in a boomerang championship in Delaware.

A Really BIG Boomerang

At almost 9 feet from tip to tip and weighing 2.3 pounds, the world's largest returning boomerang is not easy to throw. The boomerang has a handle where its two wings meet. The thrower holds the handle and hoists the boomerang on his back before launching it forward. It can fly about 75 feet.

FLYING BEFORE THE HIGHLANDER

TRY IT! Make Your Own Boomerang

What You Need
- cardboard from the back of an old cereal box
- ruler
- pencil
- scissors
- stapler

What to Do

1. Measure and cut out two 8-inch x 3/4-inch rectangles from the cardboard.

2. Place one rectangle over the other so that the two pieces are perpendicular to each other. Staple through the center where they cross. You should now have an X-shaped object with four arms.

3. Cut 1/8 inches off the side of each arm as shown.

4. Round each arm's tip.

5. To throw your boomerang, go outdoors. Holding one of the arms vertically at its tip, bring the boomerang so that it is just past your ear.

6. Then move your forearm forward, flicking your wrist as you do so and releasing the boomerang. If you don't get your boomerang to return on the first try, keep practicing until you get the hang of it.

Illustrations and photos: Colorful visuals make the words and descriptions on the page come alive.

Color border: Different color borders let you quickly see what chapter you're in.

The experiments and activities in this book require adult supervision. Time Home Entertainment Inc., Time Inc., and R studio T disclaim all responsibility and liability for any damage or injuries that may be caused or sustained while performing any of these experiments or activities.

CHAPTER ① Animals
WHAT Is a Dog's Most Powerful Sense?

You don't have to look far for the answer. It's right under your nose, or rather, a dog's nose! A dog's sense of smell is its primary way of making sense of the world. The lining inside a dog's snout is covered with scent receptors. The amount of receptors varies according to breed. A dachshund has around 125 million, while a beagle has almost twice that amount. People, by comparison, have a mere five to six million. So it's no wonder that a dog's sense of smell is so much sharper than ours.

Sniffing Around

Dogs sniff in short, rapid bursts of air, drawing scent molecules deep into nasal passageways where they collect in a nasal pocket. The molecules remain in this pocket as the dog continues to inhale and exhale until there are enough molecules for the dog to identify the odor.

A Wet Snout

The tip of a dog's snout, called the leather, is usually moist, and for a good reason. Scent molecules stick to mucous given off by glands inside a dog's nose. As the molecules dissolve, little hairs inside the nose push the scent up the nasal passageways and past the scent receptors.

Get ready to take a walk on the wild side. From man's best friend to egg-laying mammals, the world of animals holds many surprises. In this chapter, you'll meet some fascinating creatures that behave in surprising ways.

Super Smeller: The Bloodhound

The bloodhound has been called a nose with a dog attached, and that's a perfect description for a canine with 300 million scent receptors. A bloodhound's sense of smell is so sharp, its findings are used as evidence in court trials. One Kentucky bloodhound has helped law enforcement agents track down more than 600 lawbreakers.

WHAT'S More...

Researchers have trained some dogs to detect cancer in humans. The dogs can sniff out chemical changes which may signal the disease.

TRY IT!

How Well Do You Smell?

Humans don't have the smelling ability of dogs, but some people have a sharper sense of smell than others. Gather a group of your friends and take a sniff test.

What To Do:

Collect a dozen or so smelly objects from around the house. Here are some suggestions:

dried oregano or rosemary
cinnamon
cotton ball soaked
  with cologne
moth ball
mint tea bag
ripe banana peel
toothpaste
vinegar
vanilla extract
lemon slice

Have one of your friends sit and close her eyes. Place small amounts of each object under her nose. Ask her to identify the smell. Keep a list of her responses. Take turns until everyone has had a chance, including you. Which person has the best sense of smell? Were some items easier to identify than others?

WHAT Is the Jacobson's Organ in a Snake?

When a snake flicks its tongue, the reptile is probably picking up scent particles. A snake relies on its tongue and its Jacobson's organ to identify scents. Located on the roof of a snake's mouth, the Jacobson's organ is a pair of open pits loaded with sensory nerves. After the snake collects airborne chemicals on its forked tongue, it passes the tips over its Jacobson's organ, which turns the chemicals into electric signals. The signals then travel up pathways to the brain. Snakes use their Jacobson's organ to mate and to help them hunt prey.

Thanks to the Jacobson's organ, snakes can hunt by smell alone. One big reason is the forked tongue. Each tip passes over one of the two pits on the roof of its mouth, allowing the chemicals on each tip to be analyzed separately. If a prey's odor is more concentrated on one tip, the snake uses that information to figure out the direction of the animal.

Olfactory bulb (helps the snake process smells)

Tongue

Jacobson's organ

Venom gland

Chemical Messengers

Snakes aren't the only reptiles with a fully developed Jacobson's organ. Lizards, amphibians, and many mammals have this helpful sense organ. The organs are used mostly to detect chemicals called pheromones (*feh*-roh-monz). The chemicals are found in an animal's scent glands, saliva, urine, and feces (poop). They send messages to the brain, such as which animals are ready to mate, that only other members of the same species can understand.

WHAT'S More...

The Jabobson's organ was named after Ludwig Levin Jacobson, a Danish doctor and naturalist, who discovered it in 1813.

Male lions use pheromones to tell when a lioness is ready to mate. They do this by curling their upper lips into a grimace, the better to get the scent onto their Jacobson's organ.

Members of the cat family aren't the only ones to curl their lips when they are ready to mate. Horses, buffalo, zebras, and giraffes do too.

WHAT'S More...

People have a Jacobson's organ, but it is not fully developed and doesn't work as a sense organ.

Much as a snake uses its tongue, an elephant uses its "finger" at the end of its trunk to gather chemicals and bring them to its Jacobson's organ. This gives the elephant information about other elephants, such as which females are ready to mate and which males to stay away from.

WHAT Is an Aye-Aye?

With big yellow eyes set in a pointy face, large rounded ears, shaggy fur, and an extra-long middle finger that rivals E.T.'s, the aye-aye is one strange-looking creature. But what exactly is it?

Early naturalists believed the aye-aye (*eye-eye*) to be some type of rodent, possibly a squirrel, because its teeth never stopped growing. Modern scientists say the aye-aye is a primate, a close relative of the lemur. The rare and endangered aye-ayes live in the rainforests of Madagascar, an island off the southeastern coast of Africa.

What Long Fingers You Have!

An aye-aye's bony middle finger is long for a reason. It feeds on tiny insects called grubs, that live deep inside the wood of trees. To reach these tasty morsels, an aye-aye will first tap on dead wood. When the animal's sensitive ears pick up a hollow sound, it begins to gnaw the wood with its sharp teeth. Then it sticks its middle finger deep inside the hole, using its hooked claw to retrieve its meal.

Aye-ayes are nocturnal, which means they are active at night. In fact, aye-ayes are the largest nocturnal primates in the world. During the day, they sleep in round nests made out of twigs and leaves, which they build in the forks of trees.

Oh, Baby

Females give birth to one offspring at a time. The young aye-aye stays with its mother until it is around two years old, when it leaves to find its own home.

Madagascar, home to the aye-aye, is the fourth largest island in the world. This remote nation in the Indian Ocean is about the size of Texas. Up to 75 percent of the species that live on the island are endemic, which means they are unique to Madagascar, living nowhere else in the world. The aye-aye is one such species.

Happy Feet Lemurs

Another animal found only in Madagascar is the sifaka, a large lemur, a type of primate. Sifakas are most at home in trees, and usually get around by leaping from tree to tree. When they are forced to travel on the ground, they have a unique walk. With arms raised, they hop sideways on their hind legs. No wonder sifakas are also known as "dancing lemurs."

WHAT Are the Differences Between African and Asian Elephants?

Shoulders: Highest part of body

Sloped back

Flat forehead

Large ears that cover its shoulders

To most people, an elephant is an elephant—a big, grey, wrinkly animal with a long trunk. But there are actually two species of elephant: One lives in Africa and the second in Asia. Here's how you can tell them apart.

African Elephant

The largest land mammal, the African elephant weighs between 4 and 7 tons and stands up to 11 feet tall. There are two subspecies: the savannah, or bush, elephant and the forest elephant.

Both males and females have tusks.

WHAT'S More...

The Smithsonian National Museum of Natural History in Washington, DC, displays the largest known African elephant. It stands a towering 14 feet tall.

Two appendages or "fingers" at tip of trunk

The front feet have four or five toes each and the hind feet have three.

Rounded forehead with two humps on the top of its head

Head: Highest part of body

Rounded back

Small ears that don't reach over its shoulders

Asian Elephant

Smaller than its African cousin, the Asian elephant weighs between 3 and 6 tons and is around 10 feet tall. There are four subspecies: Indian, Sri Lankan, Sumatran, and Borneo.

Females don't have tusks. Only males do.

WHAT'S More...

Asian elephants were the first species of elephant to be tamed. For thousands of years, people have trained them to plow fields, haul cargo, and carry passengers.

One appendage or "finger" at tip of trunk

The front feet have five toes each and the hind feet have four.

WHAT Is a Kookaburra?

The kookaburra is a bird that lives in the forests of Australia and Papua New Guinea. It is known for its distinctive call which sounds like crazy laughter.

The bird's loud call serves two purposes. It is a way to communicate with other kookaburras and it stakes out territory, letting other birds know that it is not a good idea to move there.

The Bushman's Clock

Kookaburras are early risers, and the forests in which they live fill with their noisy shrieks each morning. They make another ruckus when they roost at night. Because of that, the birds are nicknamed the "bushman's clock." Bushmen, people who lived in the forests, could count on the birds to make noises at about the same time each morning and night—like clockwork!

Fierce Hunters

Kookaburras prey mainly on the young of other birds, insects, and snakes and other reptiles. They are fierce hunters, killing their prey by dropping them from the air or bashing them with their bills.

WHAT'S More . . .

To listen to two kookaburras calling each other, go to:
http://www.honoluluzoo.org/kookaburra.htm

WHAT Fish Communicates through Farting?

Fast Repetitive Tick (FRT) is the name scientists have given to the high-pitched buzzing sound coming out of a herring's anus. Herring, an oily fish found in the waters of the Atlantic and Pacific Oceans, travel in large schools. Scientists think that herring make the sound to communicate at night. Because most fish can't pick up the high frequency, herring can communicate their location to one another without alerting many of their predators. The exceptions are whales and dolphins. These keen-hearing mammals pick up the herring's FRTs and use the signals to hunt the fish.

Breaking Wind Underwater

Scientists believe that herring are the only fish who communicate this way. Some fish make sounds through their swim bladder, a sac located in the abdomen of certain fish. The sac keeps them from sinking. At first, scientists thought that herring used their sac to make sounds. Then researchers noticed that a stream of bubbles from the anal duct appeared at the same time as the noise.

NOISE Pollution

With so many noisy ships' engines in the oceans, noise pollution is a serious problem for many marine mammals. Killer whales that feed almost entirely on herring might not be able to hear the herring's FRTs and won't be able to hunt them as well. And noise pollution might harm the herring's ability to hear and communicate with each other.

WHAT Are Some Fish that Can Walk?

Imagine taking your pet fish for a walk! Impossible you say? A few types of fish, known as walking or ambulatory fish, can travel on land from 20 minutes to as long as several days. Some wriggle their way on land while others use arm-like fins to get around. One fish can even climb trees.

Catfish

One species of catfish can breathe air and move on land. Walking catfish get around by wriggling, much like snakes do. Native to Southeast Asia, the catfish are now found in Florida. If the fish's home dries up, it will travel on land in search of a new home. The catfish can live on land for several days—as long as their skin stays moist.

Fishzilla

Some people call the freshwater snakehead fish "Fishzilla" because its sharp teeth and long, massive body remind them of a monster. Snakeheads crawl from one pond to another by wriggling their three-foot long bodies on the ground.

Like the walking catfish, the snakehead is native to China. With no natural predators in the U.S., they can quickly take over a pond or lake, destroying the wildlife.

Mudskipper

These fish live and skip about in mud in shallow tidal pools. They use their fins like arms to move. When they are out of water, mudskippers breathe through their skin but it must be moist for them to take in oxygen. So they are never far from water.

Climbing Trees

Some mudskippers have suction-like fins on their belly. This makes it possible for them to cling to vertical surfaces, such as trees that grow in their swampy habitats.

WHAT'S
More . . .

Although it's often called the "Mexican walking fish," the axolotl (*ack*-suh-*lah*-tuhl) is not a fish at all. This aquatic salamander belongs to the amphibian family.

WHAT Is a Narwhal?

Found in Arctic waters, the narwhal is a small-toothed whale, a species closely related to the beluga. What makes the narwhal unusual is its teeth. Narwhals have two of them, but in males the larger one pushes through the upper lip and grows into a spiral tusk that can be almost nine feet in length. Female narwhals sometimes grow a tusk, but theirs is much smaller than the male's.

Unicorn of the Sea

The narwhal is most likely the basis for the legend of the unicorn. During medieval times, people believed unicorns really existed. Their proof was the tusks of narwhals that had been brought back from the Arctic by Viking sailors. These "unicorn horns" were believed to have magical properties, such as making poison harmless. Drinking cups made from the ivory tusks were worth their weight in gold.

A Whale of a Baby

Narwhals live together in groups called pods that can contain from two to hundreds of members. The pods can consist of males and females, all males, or all females. An adult male narwhal can grow to be 16 feet long and weigh up to 4,000 pounds. A female gives birth to one baby, or calf, every three years or so. The newborn weighs in at around 200 pounds and is about five feet long.

In Danger

The Inuit, people native to the Arctic, hunt the narwhal for its ivory tusk and its meat. The whale provides an important source of vitamin C in their diet. Hunters, however, are allowed to kill only a certain number of narwhals a year. The real danger to narwhals lies in climate change. The whale lives and hunts near the Arctic coast. As ice melts due to global warming, predators, such as killer whales, can move in and attack. Also, warmer weather makes chunks of ice break off. This creates more icebergs, under which narwhals can get trapped and even suffocate.

The Narwhal's TUSK

The ivory tusk that sticks out from the whale's head is flexible. It's able to bend about a foot without breaking.

What is the purpose of the tusk? Scientists aren't sure. Some think the tusk helps establish dominance over other males and, like a lion's mane or a peacock's feathers, helps attract females. Some researchers think the tusk might be a sensory organ that helps the narwhal locate food or even figure out sea temperature. But if that's true, why don't most females have tusks?

Two male narwhals cross tusks and fight, probably to impress a female.

WHAT'S More...

- About one in 500 male narwhals sport double tusks.
- The narwhal tusk is the only straight tusk in the world. Tusks of other animals, like the elephant, rhino, and walrus, are curved.
- If chipped, a tusk can sometimes repair itself.

WHAT Are Some Mammals that Lay Eggs?

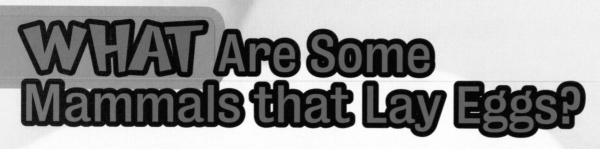

When you think of animals that lay eggs, birds, reptiles, and amphibians probably spring to mind, not mammals. Yet echidnas and platypuses, both mammals, do just that. These animals belong to a small group of mammals called monotremes. Like all mammals, monotremes are warm-blooded, have fur, and feed their young with mother's milk. But instead of giving birth to live young, monotremes lay eggs.

New Guinea

Australia

Tasmania

Echidna One and Two

There are two species of echidnas and both lay eggs. The short-beaked echidna lives in Australia and Tasmania, an island off Australia's southeast coast, while the long-beaked echidna is found in the highlands of New Guinea. After a female echidna mates, she lays an egg no bigger than a grape directly into a pouch on her abdomen. The egg hatches inside the pouch after a few weeks.

Puggles

Blind, furless, and helpless, the baby echidna, called a puggle, nurses from milk that comes from glands in the mother's skin. The newborn stays in the pouch until it grows spines, about two months later. The puggle still needs to be cared for, so the mother digs her baby a burrow and comes back to feed it until it is ready to live on its own. This happens at around seven months.

WHAT'S More ...

An echidna mother's milk is pink.

What a Puss

With its duck-like bill, flat tail, waterproof fur, and webbed feet, the platypus is one strange-looking creature. It lives in lakes and streams in Australia and Tasmania. Like echidnas, the platypus lays eggs. However, it does not have a pouch. Instead, the platypus mom-to-be digs a tunnel into the muddy banks and scoops out a "room" that she lines with leaves. She lays one or two eggs in her nest and stays curled over them until they hatch in 10 days. Like echidnas, the platypus doesn't have nipples, so her young lap up milk from patches on her abdomen. The young platypuses remain with their mother for six months before they go off on their own.

WHAT Is the Most Deadly Animal?

You might think a shark, crocodile, or man-eating tiger holds the title of world's deadliest animal. But you'd be wrong. They can't hold a candle to the humble mosquito. Yes, the pest you swat when it buzzes about your head is responsible for an estimated 2 to 3 million deaths a year. These members of the fly family spread a number of diseases, including malaria, yellow fever, and West Nile virus.

The Female of the Species

Only female mosquitoes bite. The reason? After a female mates, she needs protein from a blood meal to help her eggs develop. If she isn't developing eggs, she joins male mosquitoes in sipping on flower nectar.

How They Do It

Once a mosquito lands on her prey—that could be you—she pushes her proboscis, a long, slender tube, into the skin. Then, she locates a blood vessel and begins to suck up the blood. The blood goes up one of the two tubes in the proboscis. The other tube is used to inject the mosquito's saliva into the blood vessel. The saliva stops blood from clotting, making it flow more freely and allowing the insect enough time to drink her fill. The reason an itch develops after you've been bitten is because you're having an allergic reaction to the mosquito's saliva.

Injecting Disease

Sometimes a mosquito transmits a disease-carrying organism with its bite. The deadliest of these organisms causes malaria, a disease that kills more than 1 million people each year, mostly in Africa. There is no cure for malaria, but doctors are working on a vaccine to protect people from getting it.

Proboscis

Biting Back Against Malaria

Malaria can be prevented and treated. Unfortunately, many African nations don't have the funds to fight it. Nothing But Nets (NBN), created by the United Nations in 2006, hopes to change that by covering sleeping areas with nets. Hanging bed nets treated with insecticide is a simple yet effective way to stop mosquitoes from biting at night. So far, NBN has delivered more than 4 million nets to countries in Africa. Take that, mosquitoes!

This family in Lekki, Nigeria, will be able to sleep easy under an antimalarial bed net.

Other TOP Killers

- The **box jellyfish** is the world's most venomous, or poisonous, animal. Once stung, a victim has almost no chance of surviving unless treatment begins immediately.

- **Hippos** are super aggressive, territorial, and not the least bit afraid of humans. The combination makes them the most deadly animal in Africa after mosquitoes.

- **White-tailed deer** are gentle forest animals but more than 100 Americans die each year when their vehicles collide with them.

WHAT Is the Oldest Living Animal Species?

The granddaddy of all animal species is the horseshoe crab. A creature that resembles an armored tank, the horseshoe crab has been around for 445 million years or so, more than 200 million years before dinosaurs walked the Earth. Even more amazing, the horseshoe crab looks pretty much the same today as it did back then.

A Living Fossil

Not true crabs but close relatives to spiders, ticks, and mites, horseshoe crabs are called living fossils. If you were to compare an early fossil of the horseshoe crab to one of its living members, you wouldn't find much difference. It still has the same hinged carapace or shell, the same tail, which it uses to steer itself, and the same compound eyes, each one made up of thousands of lenses.

Living horseshoe crab

Fossil

WHAT'S More . . .

In the plant world, the ginkgo biloba holds the title of oldest species. The tree has been around for 270 million years.

Immune to Germs

How has the horseshoe crab managed to exist for so many millions of years? Scientists believe it's thanks to the creature's amazing immune system. As soon as bacteria enters the wound of an injured crab, the blood in the surrounding area immediately clots into a jell. This keeps the bacteria from moving forward so the crab won't get sick. This mysterious jell-like substance is called LAL, for short.

Medical Uses

Each year thousands of horseshoe crabs are bled to obtain LAL. The substance is then used in medical labs to test drugs that will be injected into the human bloodstream. The LAL test can quickly and accurately detect if harmful bacteria is present. Horseshoe crabs are doing their bit to keep humans safe.

Some More Living FOSSILS

- The coelacanth (*see*-luh-kanth) is the runner-up in terms of oldest living species. Fossils of this giant fish date back 410 million years.

- The chambered nautilus has lived for the last 400 million years. But today, the mollusk is in danger of dying out. Fishermen hunt the animal for its shell, which is used to make jewelry and decorations.

- Some 350 million years ago, a winged insect almost exactly like today's cockroach scurried around on Earth. These almost indestructible insects stand a good chance of being around millions of years into the future.

CHAPTER 2

Space

WHAT Is the Biggest Known Star in the Universe?

Stars come in many sizes, from small dwarfs to supergiants. Our sun is an average-size star, 870,000 miles across and big enough that one million Earths could comfortably fit inside it. But that's nothing compared to the biggest known star in the universe. VY Canis Majoris, a red supergiant with a diameter of more than 1.7 billion miles, is roughly 2,100 times the size of the sun in radius and could swallow it 8 billion times over.

A Dying Star

Images from the Hubble Space Telescope reveal that VY Canis Majoris is about to burn up. That's not too surprising since supergiants, the most massive of stars, send out energy at a much higher rate than smaller stars. While our sun will shine for about 10 billion years, supergiants last only a few million. When a supergiant finally runs out of fuel, it explodes, becoming a supernova.

Don't hold your breath waiting for VY Canis Majoris to blow up, though. Astronomers believe that probably won't happen for another 100,000 years or so. In human years that seems like a long time, but in astronomical years, it's a blink of an eye.

As it nears the end of its life, Canis Majoris puts out so much radiation that parts of its outer layers are thrown off in large outbursts. These two images, taken by the Hubble Space Telescope, show such an eruption.

Every day, scientists learn new facts about our solar system—and beyond. So fasten your seatbelts and get ready to explore the farthest reaches of the universe.

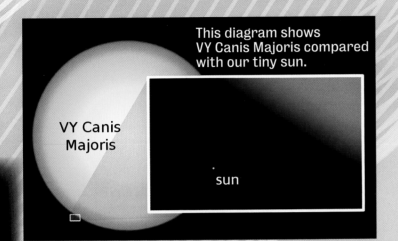

This diagram shows VY Canis Majoris compared with our tiny sun.

VY Canis Majoris

sun

WHAT'S More...

- If VY Canis Majoris took the sun's place in our solar system, its surface would extend out to Saturn's orbit.

- VY Canis Majoris is also a hypergiant, a star that is both massive and bright. It is about 450,000 times brighter than the sun.

WHAT Is the Dark Part of Space Made Of?

If you took all the stars, planets, and galaxies and combined them, they would make up just four percent of the universe. So what about the other 96 percent? The dark part of space consists of two things: dark energy and dark matter. Neither can be seen, at least not with the technology we have today. So how do scientists know they exist? Scientists figured out dark energy and dark matter are real when they studied the effects of gravity on the objects in space that we can see, such as stars and galaxies.

Dark Matter: The Glue that Holds the Universe Together

In 1933, Swiss astronomer Fritz Zwicky studied the Coma galaxy cluster and became the first to suspect that dark matter existed. He compared the galaxy's mass to its gravitational pull and noticed that the numbers weren't adding up. The combined mass of all visible matter wasn't enough to explain the force needed to hold the galaxy together. Zwicky reasoned that another kind of matter had to be at work—what he called dark matter.

The Hubble Space Telescope photographed the Coma cluster of galaxies (above), and a spiral galaxy (right).

It wasn't until 40 or so years later that scientists found more evidence that dark matter existed. In the 1970s, American astronomer Vera Rubin studied the Milky Way and other spiral galaxies. She observed that the stars in the galaxies were spinning in surprising ways, moving at a quicker speed that defied the rules of physics. She and other scientists came to believe that dark matter was providing extra gravity that caused the stars to travel so fast.

The Milky Way as seen from Earth (above, left) and from NASA's Chandra X-ray Observatory.

Dark Energy: Anti-Gravity

Dark energy, which makes up about 74 percent of the universe, is stretching the universe apart. Scientists have long known that the universe is getting bigger, with many galaxies moving farther and farther away from each other. Then in 1998, experiments showed that the rate of expansion was speeding up. Astronomers concluded that dark energy was pulling bits of matter apart. Gravity is a force that pulls objects closer. Dark energy, then, is gravity's opposite.

WHAT Is the Hottest Planet in Our Solar System?

A good guess might be Mercury, since it is the planet closest to the sun. But the correct answer is the next closest, Venus. Known as Earth's twin, Venus is similar to our planet in many ways. Both are about the same size, both have cloudy atmospheres, and both share some of the same landscape features: mountains, plains, and high plateaus. But while Earth has an average temperature of 57 degrees Fahrenheit, Venus averages a scorching 863 degrees Fahrenheit. What's more, the temperature on Venus remains constant all over the planet, and it's as hot at night as it is during the day.

Why Is Venus So Hot?

The answer lies in its thick atmosphere, the densest in our solar system. Thick yellow clouds made up of carbon dioxide blanket the planet. The clouds trap the sun's heat in Venus's atmosphere, so the planet is always hot. Many scientists believe that Venus once had oceans, just like Earth, but they evaporated.

The clouds covering Venus hide its desertlike surface.

WHAT'S More...

After our moon, Venus is the brightest object in the night sky.

WHAT Is the Only Planet in Our Solar System that Rotates on Its Side?

All the planets are tilted, but none compare to Uranus. The seventh planet from the sun has a 98-degree tilt to its axis so it rotates on its side. Instead of spinning like a top around the sun the way the other planets do, Uranus looks like a rolling ball.

What happened to make Uranus so different? Many astronomers suspect that billions of years ago something big crashed into Uranus and knocked it on its side. Another theory has to do with gravitational pull. Back when our solar system was new, the pull of gravity from other large planets might have knocked Uranus on its side.

Rotating sideways has had a big effect on the planet's seasons. Uranus orbits the sun once every 84 years. That means when its north pole points to the sun, the northern hemisphere has 42 years of sunlight. Then, it's the southern hemisphere's turn for summer and the northern side spends the next 42 years in darkness.

This illustration shows some of Uranus's rings and its sideways rotation.

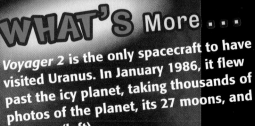

WHAT'S More . . .

Voyager 2 is the only spacecraft to have visited Uranus. In January 1986, it flew past the icy planet, taking thousands of photos of the planet, its 27 moons, and its rings (left).

WHAT Is the Largest Moon in Our Solar System?

It's fitting that the largest moon in our solar system orbits the largest planet. Ganymede measures 3,270 miles in diameter and is so big that if it orbited the sun instead of Jupiter, astronomers would classify it as a planet.

The seventh moon from Jupiter, Ganymede is larger than Mercury and one-third the size of Earth. It's named after a boy from Greek mythology who became a servant to the gods. The astronomer Galileo Galilei discovered Ganymede in 1610, along with three other moons of Jupiter. He saw the four moons for the first time through a telescope he made himself.

Jupiter

Ganymede

Ganymede's outer layer is made up of ice and rock. Scientists think it's likely that a vast ocean lies more than 100 miles below the surface.

WHAT'S More . . .

Ganymede is one of Jupiter's 63 moons. The planet has more moons than any other in our solar system.

WHAT Is the Difference Between a Comet and an Asteroid?

Both comets and asteroids are relatively small objects that orbit the sun and were formed in the early days of our solar system. But there the likeness ends. Comets, often called dirty snowballs, are made up primarily of ice with dust and rock particles mixed in. When comets draw closer to the sun, they begin to vaporize, and a halo, called a coma, forms around them. High-speed solar winds produce the long tails that give comets their distinctive look.

Asteroids come in all shapes and sizes and are composed of rock and metal, leftover scraps from when the solar system formed. Most asteroids orbit in the asteroid belt between Mars and Jupiter.

The photos of two different comets were taken by NASA spacecraft.

An artist drew a picture of an asteroid (above). The photo of another asteroid, called Vesta, was taken by NASA (right).

WHAT Is an Orrery?

An orrery (*awr*-uh-ree) is a mechanical model of the solar system that shows the positions and motions of the planets and their moons. Orreries became popular in the 17th and 18th centuries, a time when educated people became very interested in science. Then and now, people use orreries to demonstrate how the planets orbit around the sun. One early example was made for an English nobleman, the Earl of Orrery, which is how the model got its name.

Not all orreries include every one of the planets. The sun always sits in the center, but the number of planets going around it can vary. Earth usually appears, as do Mercury, Venus, Mars, and Jupiter. Some orreries include all the planets, plus some of their moons as well. Most aren't built to scale, but all the machines correctly show how the planets orbit the sun.

This painting from 1766 shows a man explaining how an orrery works.

This orrery was built in 1773. It includes all the planets that were known at the time—Mercury, Venus, Earth, Mars, Jupiter, and Saturn.

A Modern Orrery

You can see this orrery, called the Long Now, in a small museum in San Francisco, California. The model is eight feet high and shows the positions of the planets through Saturn. The orrery moves twice a day. It will take Earth 365 days to travel around the stationary sun, the same amount of time as the actual planet.

Human Orrery

In some orreries, the only moving parts are people. A famous human orrery takes place in Ireland's Armagh Observatory. On the observatory's grounds, people can stand on steel disks that mark the orbits of planets, a dwarf planet, and two comets. As visitors "orbit" the sun, they learn how the solar system works.

WHAT Is a Solar Eclipse?

Before people understood what caused a solar eclipse, they feared them. In Asia, people believed that a dragon in the sky was swallowing the sun. To scare it away, Chinese people banged on pots and pans. It worked! The sun always reappeared.

Today, we know that a solar eclipse occurs when the moon is in its new phase—the stage when the dark portion of the moon faces the Earth—and moves in front of the sun. Since the Earth, the moon, and the sun must line up in a straight line for this to happen, solar eclipses are rare.

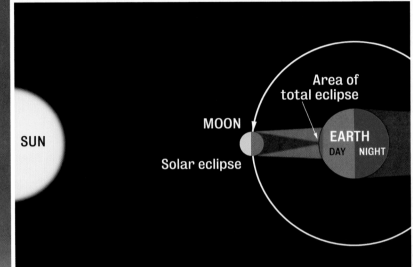

SUN

MOON

Solar eclipse

Area of total eclipse

EARTH
DAY NIGHT

As the moon creeps past the sun, the sun gradually disappears. Eventually just a small part shows. Astronomers call this the diamond ring effect. Can you guess why?

These people use special glasses to watch a solar eclipse. The glasses filter out harmful rays that can cause eye damage. Never look directly at the sun, not even during a solar eclipse.

Create a Solar Eclipse

What You Need

- Straw
- Scissors
- Quarter
- Orange
- Flashlight

What to Do

1. Cut a slit in the straw and insert the coin.

2. If you're a righty, hold the straw in your right hand, pick up the orange with your left hand. If you're a lefty, do the opposite.

3. Position the two objects in a line about 8 inches apart.

4. Ask a friend or family member to shine the flashlight from behind the quarter.

5. Observe the shadow the coin (moon) casts on the orange (Earth).

6. Note how the coin blocks the light and casts a shadow on the orange. The darker central shadow, the umbra, shows a total eclipse. The lighter outer area, the penumbra, shows a partial eclipse.

WHAT'S More...

Sometimes the Earth moves directly between the sun and the moon. When this happens, it's called a lunar eclipse.

WHAT Is a Blue Moon?

A blue moon isn't blue at all. It's the name given to the second full moon in a calendar month. Two moons in one month don't happen all that often. Most years have 12 full moons, one appearing each month. But once every three years or so, an extra moon slips in. That's because our calendar is based on the amount of time it takes Earth to orbit the sun and not on the lunar month, which is 29½ days.

This definition of a blue moon is a modern one and it came about by mistake. Before 1946, the *Farmers' Almanac* said a blue moon was the third full moon in a season that has four full moons. A writer for an astronomy magazine misunderstood the meaning and wrote that a blue moon was the second full moon in a month. This meaning stuck. In 1999, the error was discovered. But since more than 50 years had passed, most people continue to call the second moon in a month a blue moon.

Full Moon Names

Many cultures around the world gave names to each month's full moon. Here are the names from North America's Algonquin tribes. European settlers later adopted many of the names.

MONTH	FULL MOON NAME
January	Wolf Moon
February	Snow Moon
March	Worm Moon
April	Pink Moon
May	Flower Moon
June	Strawberry Moon
July	Buck Moon
August	Sturgeon Moon
September	Harvest Moon
October	Hunter's Moon
November	Beaver Moon
December	Cold Moon

WHAT'S More . . .

The expression "once in a blue moon" means something that happens rarely, just like two full moons in one month.

WHAT Is Earth's Largest Meteorite?

In 1920, a farmer was turning over the soil in a field in Namibia, in southwestern Africa, when his plow hit an obstacle. When it was dug up, the large mass of metal turned out to be the largest meteorite ever found. The Hoba (*hoe*-bah) meteorite, named after the farm where it was discovered, weighs more than 60 tons. It is about 9 feet long, 9 feet wide, and 3 feet thick. It's 84 percent iron and 16 percent nickel, with trace amounts of other metals. Scientists estimate that it fell to Earth around 80,000 years ago.

Runner-Up

The Cape York meteorite is the world's second largest, weighing in at 34 tons. It hit Earth some 10,000 years ago, landing in Greenland. Robert Peary, the famous Arctic explorer, discovered the meteorite in 1894. Like the Hoba, the Cape York is made up of iron and nickel. Unlike the Hoba, it didn't stay where it landed. Peary hauled the big chunk of metal to New York City. You can see—and touch—it at the American Museum of Natural History.

WHAT Was the Space Shuttle?

From TIME FOR KIDS

Thirty years ago, space travel was far from routine. Back then, only a handful of Americans had traveled to space, and they had done so on spacecraft that could only be used once. At the end of the voyage, the crafts would parachute into the ocean, never to be flown again.

All of that changed when NASA rolled out its first space shuttle in 1981. The new spacecraft was designed to blast off using rocket boosters, orbit the Earth, and land like a plane—over and over again.

Shuttle Highs and Lows

In the last 30 years, NASA's five shuttles have completed more than 130 missions. They have helped the agency achieve many goals, from launching flying telescopes to helping to build the International Space Station (ISS), a floating space lab in the sky. The program has also seen its share of darker days. Fourteen lives were tragically lost in two shuttle accidents. After each disaster, NASA paused the shuttle program.

SHUTTLE HISTORY

Here are some of the most important events in the shuttle's past.

1980

April 12, 1981
The first shuttle craft, *Columbia*, lifts off, carrying two astronauts.

June 18, 1983
Challenger sails into orbit with Sally Ride. She is the first U.S. woman in space. Two months later, Guion Bluford becomes the first African American to travel into space.

February 7, 1984
An untethered astronaut spacewalks for the first time.

January 28, 1986
Seven crew members lose their lives when *Challenger* explodes shortly after liftoff. NASA suspends flights for nearly three years.

1990

April 24, 1990
Discovery launches the Hubble Space Telescope. Scientists soon realize that there is a defect in Hubble's main mirror, causing pictures to come out blurry.

The *Endeavour* is one of the five shuttles retired from the space program.

The End of an Era

On July 21, 2011, the space shuttle *Atlantis* concluded its final mission, marking the end of the space shuttle program. The U.S. government says the space vehicles are too old and too costly to operate. Instead of soaring into space, the shuttles will be on display in museums. And NASA astronauts will be left without a ride of their own. For now, to reach ISS, they will have to pay to travel aboard Russian spacecraft. Due to recent budget cuts in the space program, NASA scientists suspect that U.S. astronauts might be hitchhiking to space for some time.

2000

2010

December 2, 1993
Endeavour takes a crew to repair Hubble's mirror. After days of work, Hubble is fixed.

October 29, 1998
John Glenn, who in 1962 became the first American to orbit Earth, returns to space aboard *Discovery*. At 77, he is the oldest space traveler.

December 6, 1998
Endeavour delivers the first U.S. piece of the International Space Station.

February 1, 2003
Seven astronauts lose their lives as *Columbia* returns to Earth. The shuttle breaks apart minutes before it is expected to land. NASA suspends flights for more than two years.

July 21, 2011
Atlantis commmpletes its final mission. NASA retires its shuttle program.

WHAT Is a Space Probe?

Thanks to space probes, we know a lot more about space than ever before. Space probes are unmanned spacecraft that explore the solar system, taking detailed photos and gathering information about heavenly bodies. Space probes might fly past planets, orbit around them, or land on them. Once a probe is inside the planet's atmosphere or has landed, instruments on board conduct experiments. The information is then relayed back to Earth for scientists to study.

A *Viking* lander on Mars

Mars Touchdowns

The first probe to successfully land on Mars touched down in 1976. The two *Viking* landers relayed to Earth the first color images of the planet's rusty surface. The landers also scooped up soil samples and tested them for evidence of life forms. The results came back negative, but scientists are hopeful that future probes might prove different.

In 2004, twin rovers *Spirit* and *Opportunity* landed on Mars and set about exploring, returning more than 100,000 images. They've also conducted geological tests on samples of rocks and soil. In 2009, the rovers uncovered evidence of water on Mars.

Engineers designed the rovers to run for just a few months, but they surprised everyone by lasting for years. In 2010, *Spirit* became trapped in sand (photo). *Opportunity* was still going strong in early 2012.

Voyager 1 and 2

Launched in 1977, *Voyager 1* and *2* are still flying through space on a mission to explore the outer limits of our solar system. Along the way, the twin space probes took time to study the outer planets. *Voyager 1* flew past Jupiter and Saturn, sending back images. Then the probe continued its journey deeper into space. It has now traveled more than 10.5 billion miles and is the farthest man-made object from Earth.

    Voyager 2 took a grand tour of the outer solar system, visiting Jupiter, Uranus, and Neptune. It is set to enter interstellar space in 2015.

    Each spacecraft carries a disk (photo, right), that contains images and sounds from Earth, including greetings in 55 languages to any life-form it may meet.

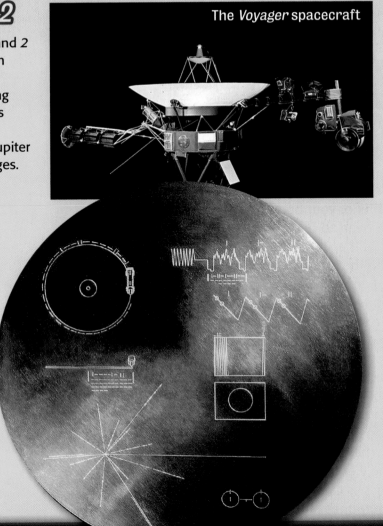

The *Voyager* spacecraft

New Horizons

On its journey to Pluto, the spacecraft *New Horizons* sailed past Jupiter in 2007, one year after it rocketed into space. The probe sent back images never before seen, such as lightning near Jupiter's poles and huge clumps of matter racing past the planet's rings. *New Horizons* is expected to reach Pluto by 2015.

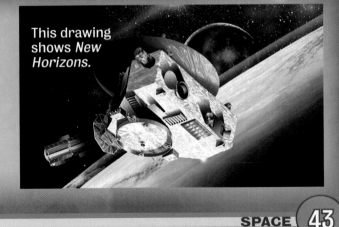

This drawing shows *New Horizons*.

WHAT Is the Brain Made Of?

Your brain is the commander-in-chief of your body. It tells your heart to beat, your lungs to breathe, and your eyes to blink. The human brain is the most complex human organ. Billions of nerve cells, called neurons, make up the brain. These neurons are connected, constantly interacting with each other as they send messages to all the cells in the body.

If you look at a neuron up close, you can see that it branches off into lots of long spindly ends. One extra-long branch is called the axon. The shorter ones are dendrites. These nerve endings connect to other neurons, passing on and receiving information in the form of electrical signals. The axon sends out signals, while the dendrites receive signals from other neurons.

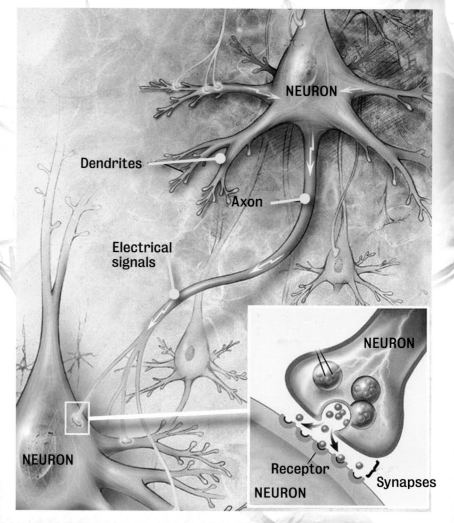

Neurons don't touch one another. Instead they connect by jumping across synapses, tiny gaps between the cells. A synapse releases chemicals that travel across a gap and trigger an electrical impulse in the next neuron.

Is your funny bone really funny—and is it even a bone? What's your gluteus maximus and what's it good for? You'll find out in this chapter as you get to know the ins and outs of your body.

The outer part of the brain, called the cerebral cortex, is grayish in color and has deep folds. This area, where most of our thinking takes place, is extremely dense with dendrites.

The inner area of the brain is paler in color and known as white matter. It's mostly made up of axons. Axons are covered with a fatty substance called myelin sheath, which gives the inner brain its whitish color.

WHAT'S More...

Because it doesn't have pain receptors, the brain can't feel pain.

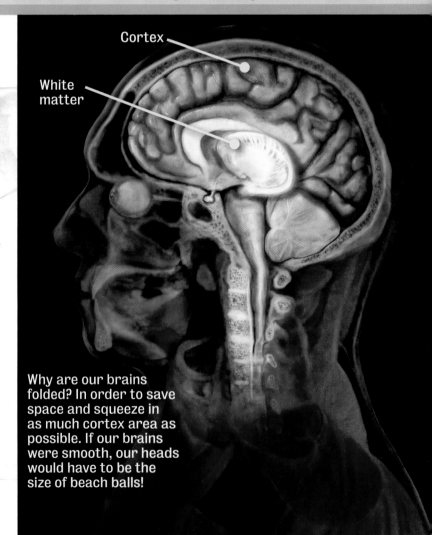

Cortex

White matter

Why are our brains folded? In order to save space and squeeze in as much cortex area as possible. If our brains were smooth, our heads would have to be the size of beach balls!

Human Brain Stats

Weight: about 3 pounds

Size: about the size of your two fists put together

Surface area: about four sheets of letter-size paper

Number of neurons: 100 billion

WHAT Are Some Ways People Learn?

There's more than one kind of smart. There are eight! At least according to Dr. Howard Gardner, a Harvard professor who came up with the idea of Multiple Intelligence or MI. He says that people learn and show their intelligence in many ways. Many scientists now agree with him.

MI is divided into eight different ways of learning. People have ability in all the intelligences, but in different amounts. Take a look at the different kinds of smarts listed below and see if you can figure out how you learn best.

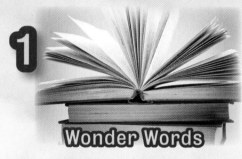

1 Wonder Words

You're good with words. You enjoy reading, writing, and word games. You may find that learning a foreign language will be easy—and fun—for you.

2 Number One Numbers

Calculating math problems come easily to you. You see patterns everywhere. You probably ace science and math tests.

3 High Notes

You have no trouble picking out a tune's melody or rhythm. You might like to sing, play an instrument, and listen to all kinds of music.

4 Seeing Is Learning

You enjoy looking at interesting objects and possibly have a talent for design. Many artistic people, such as painters, photographers, and architects, have spatial intelligence—they can visualize how things look or work in their mind.

5 Hands On

Are you good at sports? Do you pick up dance steps easily? Or perhaps you're good with your hands and like to make things. People with this kind of intelligence learn by doing.

7 Getting To Know You

You make friends easily, you're interested in finding out what makes people tick. Psychologists and salespeople have these skills.

6 Me, Myself, and I

You're someone who tends to look inward. You know yourself very well, and regularly take stock of your likes and dislikes, your talents, what you're good at doing—and not so good at doing!

8 The Great Outdoors

You love nature. You're interested in knowing the names of plants and animals. You could spend hours gazing at a waterfall or observing a bird build its nest. You may keep a rock collection or be involved in environmental causes.

WHAT Is Dyslexia?

Turn this book upside down and hold it up to a mirror. Now try to read the words. With the letters flipped and reversed, it's very difficult—if not impossible. Many people with dyslexia see words on the page this way. Certain letters might look backwards or upside down. Or the words might appear blurry or seem to "jump" around.

Dyslexia is a condition that affects a person's ability to read, write, spell, and listen. Someone with dyslexia has a hard time making the connection between the way letters look and the sounds of words. Though learning may be more difficult for kids with dyslexia, it doesn't mean that they aren't smart. It means they have trouble processing what they see, hear, or write, into meaningful information.

What Causes Dyslexia?

Scientists believe a glitch in the brain's wiring makes decoding language difficult for some people. Although there is no cure for it, some experts think that if caught early, dyslexia can be reversed. One way to do this is by teaching readers to sound out words, build up vocabulary, and to practice reading. Many dyslexic people discover their own solutions, such as listening to books on tape or asking for extra time to complete tests.

WHAT'S More...

Studies indicate that 17 percent of the U.S. population has dyslexia.

The owl was a bird.

Teh owl saw a brid.

The owl was

Some kids with dyslexia reverse the order of letters in a word.

Tom Cruise

As a student looks at a letter, he hears and writes it at the same time. This is one way that kids with dyslexia learn to read.

People with dyslexia might experience one or more difficulties reading. Letters that look similar might appear as reversed. For instance, a *b* might look like a *d,* or a *p* like a *q.* Or the letters might appear to swirl about on the page, in constant motion. Words may appear incorrectly spaced, with either too much space between letters and words or not enough, with all the letters squished together.

Thew ord sare n otsp aced cor rect ly.

We spell wrds xatle az tha snd to us.

Sometimesallthelettersarepushedtogether.

Famous People with Dyslexia

Many successful people have dyslexia. Here are a just a few.

Jay Leno, late-night talk show host

Whoopi Goldberg, actor

Keira Knightley, actor

Tom Cruise, actor

Jewel, singer

Steven Spielberg, director

Muhammad Ali, boxer

WHAT Is the Strongest Muscle in Your Body?

Of the more than 600 muscles in the human body, which one deserves the title of strongest? The answer isn't simple. It all depends on how you define strength. Some muscles have greater endurance or work harder, but when it comes to pure brute force, one muscle rules. Chew on this—it's the jaw muscle. The human jaw can chomp down with a force of up to 200 pounds. It would be the same as having a 200-pound weight coming down on an object. In theory, the jaw is capable of crushing its own teeth.

The Winner: The Jaw Muscle!

Here Are Some Other Winners:

Pump It Up

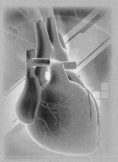

The heart, which works 24/7, is the body's hardest-working muscle. With each heartbeat, it pumps 2 ounces of blood and at least 2,500 gallons of blood daily.

Always Moving

Among the smallest muscles in the body, the eye muscles are also some of the strongest. They have great elastic strength and can exert force quickly. When reading, your eyes make more than 10,000 tiny movements per hour.

Tongue Twister

Another tough worker is the tongue. Actually a group of muscles, the tongue never quits. It's at work when we eat, speak, and sleep. That's right. At night while we snooze, the tongue pushes saliva into the throat. If you want to see how strong it is, try forcing your tongue down with your finger.

Be Seated

The gluteus maximus—the muscles in the butt—is the body's largest muscle and one of its strongest. It keeps your trunk (the main part of the body from the stomach up to the head) erect.

Muscle Men

Bodybuilders work hard at developing their muscles. They pump them up using weight-training exercises that slowly get heavier. They follow a special diet that includes a lot of protein, and they get plenty of rest between workouts. Exercise causes the body's muscles to tear ever so slightly. During recovery, the body repairs these tears, allowing the muscles to grow bigger.

WHAT Is an Adam's Apple?

Ever wonder why your dad's voice is lower and deeper than your mom's? It's mostly thanks to his Adam's apple, that telltale bump on the front of a man's neck. An Adam's apple is made of cartilage, the same flexible substance found in your nose. As a boy gets older, his larynx (*lar*-inks), or voice box, starts to get bigger and the surrounding cartilage grows and hardens with it. In some men, the cartilage sticks out and becomes a bump you can see. That's the Adam's apple.

Why That Name

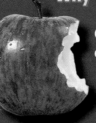

The Bible tells about the Garden of Eden, and Adam eating the apple that Eve gave him. To many people, the bump in a man's throat looks like a piece of the swallowed fruit.

Name That Tune

Your vocal chords are muscles inside your larynx. The shorter chords produce high sounds, while the longer ones make lower sounds. As boys and girls grow, so do their voice boxes and vocal chords. Boys' grow bigger, so their voices end up lower and deeper.

WHAT'S More . . .

Because the larynx grows so quickly as a boy matures, his voice sometimes breaks or cracks. After a few months, this stops.

WHAT Is the Funny Bone?

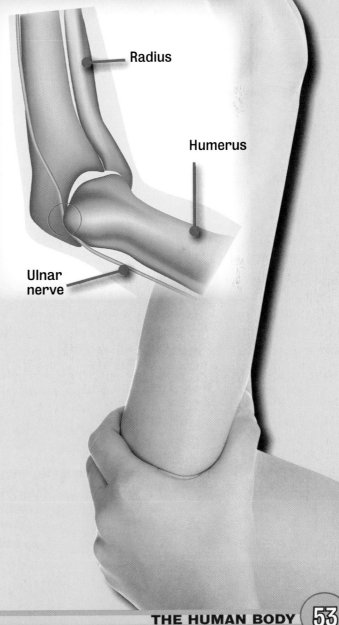

Radius

Humerus

Ulnar nerve

Bang! If you've ever hit your elbow in a certain spot, you know that there's nothing funny about the funny bone. In fact, it isn't a bone at all, but a nerve, the ulnar nerve to be exact. The nerve runs from the hand to the shoulder.

Just above the elbow, along the inside of the arm, is a spot where the nerve is exposed. Unlike other nerves, which are protected by muscles or bones, the ulnar nerve is covered only by skin. That's why when we bump or bang this delicate spot, we feel pain.

So why is it called a funny bone? Many people report feeling a weird, tingly feeling when they hit the nerve. Or perhaps it's because the funny bone is next to the arm's humerus (*hoo*-muh-rus) bone, which sounds a lot like the word "humorous".

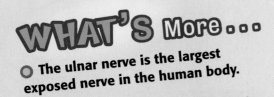

- The ulnar nerve is the largest exposed nerve in the human body.

- The ulnar nerve controls feeling in your fourth and fifth fingers and in the back of your hand.

WHAT Does It Mean To Be Double-Jointed?

A joint, the place where two bones meet, allows your body to move. Without hip and knee joints, you'd walk around as stiff-legged as Frankenstein's monster or the Tin Man in *The Wizard of Oz*.

So, do double-jointed people have twice as many joints? Not at all. They have the same number as everyone else. It's just that they can bend their joints more than the average person. In some cases, a lot more.

Most joints have a set range of motion. They can only go so far. Some people, though, have a much larger range of motion than others. These contortionists seem to have bones made out of rubber. They can bend and shape their arms and legs into incredible positions.

Circus performers and gymnasts develop great flexibility.

WHAT'S More...

As people age, their bones and ligaments harden. That's why children are more flexible than most adults.

What enables a person to turn into a shape that looks like a pretzel? It helps to know a little about how joints work. Some, like the joints in your knees, swing back and forth, much the way a hinge allows a door to open and close. Other joints, like those in your neck, pivot and let you turn your head. Ball-and-socket joints work yet another way. The rounded end of a bone (the ball) fits inside the hollowed end (the socket) of another, allowing the bone to move front to back and side to side. The joints in your shoulders and hips work this way.

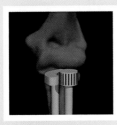

Hinge joint

Pivot joint

Ball–and–socket joint

What a Joint

People who are double-jointed don't have deep sockets, so the ball part rests shallowly in the socket. This helps joints rotate in any direction. Double-jointed people also have more flexible ligaments (tissue that holds bones together) and tendons (tissue that attaches muscles to bones).

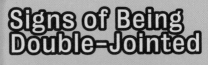

Signs of Being Double-Jointed

○ From a standing position, you can touch the floor with the palms of your hands without bending your knees.

○ You can bend your fingers all the way back until they almost touch your wrist.

CHAPTER ④ Weather & Climate

WHAT Is the Driest Place on Earth?

Arica, a city in Chile in South America, once went 14 years without a single drop of rain. The average amount of precipitation that falls is a measly 0.03 inches. Arica is located in the world's driest desert—the Atacama.

The desert covers more than 600 miles. In this desolate area, you won't see plants or animals, just vast stretches of empty land. One region has soil that is similar to the kind found on Mars. In fact, sci-fi directors sometimes film in the Atacama.

You can see snow-capped Andes Mountains from the bone-dry Atacama Desert.

Weather is what it's like outside from day to day. Climate is weather over a long period of time. Check out both climate and weather facts on these pages.

CHILE

Plants in the Atacama Desert get the water they need by taking in moisture from fog.

Even though the Atacama Desert is such a harsh environment, there are towns and farms. How do people survive? Some communities transported water by truck, but that was very expensive. Today, they make use of a marine fog called *camanchaca* (ka-men-*chak*-a). Scientists found a way to collect the dense fog that forms on Chile's Pacific coast and drifts inland over the desert. People hang netting, which captures the water droplets in the fog. The droplets condense and drip into basins. The water is then piped to villages in the area. In the village of Chungungo, this system supplies the residents with more than 2,500 gallons of water each day.

Nets like these help collect water droplets in the fog.

WHAT Are the Most Extreme Daytime Temperatures Ever Recorded?

Aziziya, a city in Libya in Africa, has had many hot days. None were as blazing as the one on September 12, 1922, when the temperature rose to 136 degrees Fahrenheit, the highest ever recorded on Earth.

Hot Spot

In North America, Death Valley in California tops the heat charts. On July 10, 1913, the temperature reached a scorching 134 degrees Fahrenheit, the hottest ever recorded in the Western Hemisphere. During July, Death Valley has an average daily high of 115 degrees. At night, it cools down to a practically chilly 87 degrees!

Brrrrr

July 21, 1983, was an especially cold day in Antarctica. At the Russian research station there, the thermometer dipped to minus 128.6 degrees Fahrenheit, the lowest temperature ever recorded on Earth.

WHAT Are Some Weather Myths?

It can't snow when the temperature is above freezing.

It can, if conditions are just right. Snowflakes form high up in the atmosphere whenever the temperature is at or below freezing. If, as they fall, they hit air that is above freezing, the flakes will start to melt. If the air is dry enough, the melting liquid cools the air surrounding the flakes (in the same way that sweating cools down our skin) and keeps the snowflakes from melting completely.

Lightning never strikes the same place twice.

Some places get hit again and again, especially if it's an object that's tall or is in an isolated setting, such as a lone tree in a field. The Empire State Building in New York City is hit more than 20 times a year.

A raindrop is shaped like a tear.

Raindrops start out as round droplets. As they fall, small raindrops under 0.03 inch stay round. Larger ones take on the shape of a hamburger bun, flat on the bottom and curved on top. Really large raindrops, those more than 0.17 inch in diameter, break apart and form two smaller drops. Tiny raindrops keep their round shape thanks to surface tension, the water's "skin" that makes molecules stick together. Larger drops, though, fall at a greater speed, so air pressure pushes against the base of the drop causing it to flatten.

WHAT Are the Northern Lights?

The areas around the Arctic Circle and the North Pole are the best viewing spots for one of nature's most spectacular light shows, the aurora borealis (ah-*roar*-uh bore•ee-*al*-is) or Northern Lights. Dazzling lights flicker and shift across the sky. Beginning as a sliver-green arc, this curtain of light ripples across the sky flickering, glowing, and shifting in shades of green, yellow, pink, red, blue, and purple.

What causes this fantastic display? The answer begins with the sun. Solar flare explosions shoot off particles of electrons and protons, some of which are carried away by solar wind. Traveling at speeds of more than 600,000 miles per hour, some of the particles eventually reach Earth. The Earth's magnetic fields tug at the energy-charged particles, pulling them into our planet's atmosphere. There they meet up with the main gases in our atmosphere, oxygen and nitrogen. The collision causes the gases to light up and glow in a profusion of color.

People living in Iceland are often treated to light shows.

The crew aboard the International Space Station
took this picture of the aurora borealis.

WHAT'S
More . . .

The aurora borealis
gets its name from two
gods—Aurora, the Roman
goddess of dawn, and
Boreas, the Greek god of
the north wind.

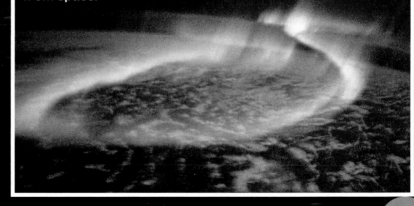

The South Pole has its own light display. However, the
aurora australis usually appears over unpopulated areas
so few people ever get to see it. This photo was taken
from space.

WHAT Is a Monsoon?

Which way does the wind blow? In India and much of Asia, the answer determines whether the land will be wet or dry. In winter, northeasterly winds bring warm, dry air for about six months. Then, around May, the wind pattern shifts, and moist southwesterly winds from the Indian Ocean cause heavy rains that drench the land. The heavy storms last six months before the dry air returns.

A monsoon, then, is a wind pattern that reverses with the seasons. There are two kinds of monsoons, dry and wet, and both can be extremely dangerous, although in very different ways.

Wet and Dry

During the wet monsoon, heavy rains sweep the land, causing flooding and landslides. In parts of India, rain dumps more than 400 inches of water. Although the wet monsoon can cause much damage, people need the rains to live. Without the storms, which bring as much as 90 percent of rainfall in a year, crops would die and people would go hungry.

When the winds shift again, the dry season returns. The land becomes parched. Heat waves and droughts are common.

In 2011, Pakistan was affected by heavy flooding due to monsoons.

Rickshaws and people wade through the flooded streets in a town in India.

Too Much Rain

Cherrapunji, India, is one of the wettest places on Earth, yet it can go months without rainfall. During the dry monsoon season, villagers struggle to find drinkable water. Once the rainy season comes, Cherrapunji is drenched. The town averages 463 inches a year. One year, more than 900 inches of rain fell, almost all of it during the rainy season.

When the dry season returns after a monsoon, it can cause damage to crops.

WHAT'S More...

○ Monsoon comes from the Arabic word mausim, meaning "season."

○ Although monsoons are worse in Asia, other parts of the world also get these seasonal winds. Monsoons occur over large areas of land from Australia to the Caribbean Sea.

WHAT Is Acid Rain?

Most people think that rain is pure, clean water. But even clean rain contains some acid, though not enough to cause harm.

Acid rain, however, has way more acid than clean rain. In fact, some drops are almost as acidic as vinegar. Acid rain doesn't even have to be rain. It can be any precipitation, such as snow, sleet, or fog, that has unusually high amounts of acid.

Rain Pollution

Acid rain is caused by air pollution. The coal, oil, and natural gas we burn to run power plants, factories, homes, and vehicles, release gases into the air. Two in particular, sulfur dioxide and nitrogen oxide, are especially dangerous, at least when they combine with water vapor to become sulfuric acid or nitric acid.

Acid rain damages the environment, washing away nutrients in soil. It can kill fish and other marine life. Acid rain even harms buildings as it dissolves minerals in stone.

Acid rain killed the spruce trees in this forest.

Chemicals in acid rain can kill fish and other marine life such as salamanders.

Good News

The good news is that efforts to combat acid rain are working. In 1990, the Clean Air Act required power plants to reduce the amount of sulfur dioxide they released into the atmosphere. Today, pollution levels are lower. Lakes that were once too acidic for fish are now teeming with life. Forests are coming back as well. But the work is far from over and more efforts will be needed to help reduce acid rain even further.

Statues and monuments, like the Egyptian obelisk above, show signs of corrosion due to acid rain.

The pH Scale

Scientists measure acidity on a pH scale that goes from zero all the way up to 14. The stronger the acid, the lower its pH. Battery acid, for instance, is 0 on the scale. Tomato juice is 5. A solution that measures 7, such as distilled water, is right in the middle. It isn't acid at all. Neither is it alkaline, the opposite of acid. Liquid drain cleaner, an alkaline, tops the scale at 14.

Unpolluted rain has a pH rating of 5.6, just a bit more than the amount found in a banana. To be considered acid rain, the water must measure 5 or less on the scale.

A scientist collects pollutants to determine the effects of acid rain.

WHAT Is the Northeast Passage?

Adolf Erik Nordenskiold

Who doesn't love a shortcut? For centuries people in Russia looked for a northern route from the Atlantic to the Pacific Ocean. The obvious way was to travel by sea along the northern coast of Russia. Unfortunately, this "climate-controlled" path lies in frigid Arctic waters and is frozen solid much of the year. It wasn't until 1878 that Adolf Erik Nordenskiold, a Finnish-Swedish explorer, made the first successful crossing through what is known as the Northeast Passage.

The passage is a shipping lane that runs from the North Pacific Ocean through the Bering Strait and the Arctic Ocean to the North Atlantic Ocean and Europe (see map). The route gave traders a shortcut between Europe and Asia. It shaved thousands of miles off the usual route through the Suez Canal in Egypt. The trouble was that ships could never make it through the passage in winter. Even during the summer months, floating ice made trips too dangerous for regular travel.

Icebreakers Pave the Way

Now, that's beginning to change. Global warming is shrinking the ice in the Arctic, and this is opening new lanes in the Northeast Passage. Ships still can't sail during winter months without the help of icebreakers. During summer, though, routes near the shore are becoming increasingly ice-free and more ships are passing through. Commercial shippers save money on these shorter trips because they spend much less on fuel.

Icebreakers are used to open sea lanes in the Northeast Passage.

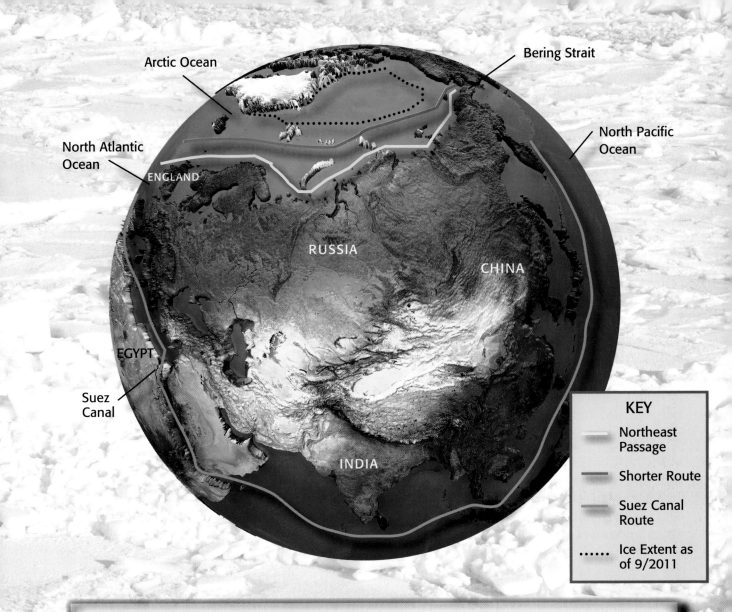

Arctic Ocean

Bering Strait

North Atlantic Ocean

North Pacific Ocean

ENGLAND

RUSSIA

CHINA

EGYPT

Suez Canal

INDIA

KEY

— Northeast Passage

— Shorter Route

— Suez Canal Route

...... Ice Extent as of 9/2011

What Is Global Warming?

The Earth's average temperature is gradually rising. Year by year it is heating up. By 2100, many scientists predict that our planet's overall temperature will be from 2 to 11.5 degrees Fahrenheit higher than it is today. That might not sound like much, but only a difference of 9 degrees Fahrenheit separates our time from the Ice Age.

Why is Earth getting hotter? Many scientists think burning fossil fuels, such as gasoline and coal, are to blame. The fuels give off carbon dioxide which rises into the atmosphere. This traps the sun's heat so it can't escape back into space. Global warming disrupts the climate and its weather patterns.

WHAT Is a Dust Devil?

It's a clear, sunny day with no clouds in the sky. Suddenly you spot a swirling column of air headed toward you. Is it a tornado? No, it's a dust devil, a whirlwind that you can see because it picks up dust and other debris from the ground.

Compared to tornadoes, dust devils are small, usually 10 to 15 feet around and from 100 to 400 feet high. Unlike most tornadoes, a dust devil lasts about a minute or so, with wind speeds under 50 miles per hour. Every once in a while, a more powerful dust devil forms. The largest can reach 300 feet across, last up to an hour, and travel at 60 miles per hour. Occasionally, dust devils can cause damage and injury.

Desert Dust Devils

Dust devils most often form in deserts and other wide-open places where the ground heats up until it is very hot. If this hot air rises and meets cooler air, the air may start to spin faster and faster. A dust devil will form if light winds tilt spinning air upright. Once vertical, the dust devil takes off, careening across the landscape. As more hot air feeds into the bottom of the whirlwind, the dust devil grows larger and spins faster. As soon as cooler air is sucked inside, the dust devil collapses.

WHAT'S More...

After Mount St. Helens erupted in 1980, people could see hundreds of sand devils that had formed from volcanic ash spin across the bare landscape.

Comparing Tornadoes and Dust Devils

TORNADO	DUST DEVIL
forms from thunderclouds	forms from the ground up
forms over wooded or plains area	forms over deserts
can be up to 2,000 feet high	can be up to 400 feet high
can spin up to 250 miles per hour	can spin up to 60 miles per hour
rotates counter-clockwise	rotates clockwise
lasts from 10 minutes up to an hour	lasts a few minutes

Martian Dust Devils

Dust devils swirl across the Red Planet, too, and they form there the same way they do on Earth. The Martian whirlwinds, though, are much, much larger than any on our planet—up to 50 times as wide and more than two miles high. Because dust devils are common on Mars, they could damage expensive equipment on NASA probes there. So far, this hasn't been a problem. Both the *Spirit* and *Opportunity* rovers on Mars met up with dust devils and came away with their solar panels cleaned! This greatly increased their power levels and extended the robots' usefulness.

WHAT Is an Anemometer?

The anemometer is a handy instrument used to measure wind speed. There are many kinds, but the simplest is the cup anemometer, invented in 1846 by John Thomas Romney Robinson, an Irish astronomer and meteorologist. This type of anemometer has four arms attached to the top of a pole. At the end of each arm is a cup, positioned to catch the wind. When the wind blows, the cups spin around the pole. Modern anemometers have an electrical device that records the cups' revolutions and calculates wind speed.

Other Types of Anemometers

One of Robinson's anemometers (right), and a modern version (below).

A windmill anemometer gives the wind's direction, as well as its speed.

Laser Doppler anemometers work by figuring out how much light from a laser beam is reflected off moving particles of air.

An ultrasound anemometer uses sound waves to determine wind speed.

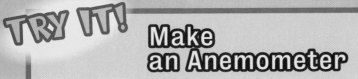

Make an Anemometer

What You Need

- 2 strips of cardboard, 1 inch x 12 inches
- stapler
- 4 aluminum foil baking cups
- sharpened pencil with an eraser
- permanent colored markers and/or stickers
- lump of clay, flattened at base
- push pin
- watch with a minute hand

What to Do

1. Cross the cardboard strips in the shape of an X and staple at the center.

2. Decorate one of the baking cups with markers and/or stickers so that it stands out from the others.

3. Staple the cups to the cardboard frame, as shown. Make sure the open ends all face the same direction.

4. Push the sharp end of the pencil into the clay. Push the pin through the center of the cardboard frame and into the pencil's eraser.

5. Take your anemometer outside on a windy day and secure it on a flat surface. Record the number of revolutions it makes per minute by counting the decorated cup each time it passes you.

Note: While your model anemometer can't give you an exact wind speed, you can see how fast the wind is blowing by observing how rapidly the cups are turning.

CHAPTER 5 Food

WHAT Is the Difference Between a Fruit and a Vegetable?

Pumpkins, apples, peaches, cucumbers. Which are fruits and which are vegetables? It may seem like an easy question, but the scientific answer may surprise you.

To a botanist (a scientist who studies plants), they're all fruits. A fruit is the part of a plant that grew from a flower. It contains seeds that can turn into a new plant. The seed can be a single large one, as in an avocado, or they can be many small ones, the kind you find in a cucumber, squash, or an orange.

What is a vegetable? Vegetables are the parts of a plant that you can eat. You can eat the roots (carrots), tubers (potatoes), leaves (spinach), or stems (celery). So the next time an adult tells you to eat your squash because vegetables are good for you, you can say, "You mean eat your fruit!"

Have you ever eaten a bug? What about sheep intestines? Throughout history, people have dined on a wide variety of foods. Expand your palate and learn more about some tasty tidbits.

TRY IT!

According to scientists, which of the following are fruits and which are vegetables? The answers are upside down below.

1. Cantaloupe
2. Zucchini
3. Lettuce
4. Coconut
5. Asparagus
6. Eggplant
7. Turnip
8. Olive
9. Corn
10. Cabbage

Fruits: 1, 2, 4, 6, 8, 9; Vegetables: 3, 5, 7, 10

Seeing RED: Tomatoes Go to Court

According to scientists, tomatoes are fruits because they have seeds. But thanks to a 1893 U.S. Supreme Court decision, tomatoes are vegetables.

The Court ruled that it didn't matter what scientists said. People think of tomatoes as vegetables and eat them with the main part of dinner. Fruits, the Court said, are eaten as dessert. Since nobody has a tomato for dessert, well then, it's got to be a vegetable.

WHAT'S More...

In 1987, Arkansas named the tomato the official state fruit *and* the official state vegetable.

WHAT Are Nutrients?

You have just finished eating a peanut butter and jelly sandwich. As your body digests the meal, the bread, peanut butter, and jelly are broken down into carbohydrates, fats, protein, vitamins, minerals, and water. These nutrients, substances found in food that you need to live, are then absorbed into your bloodstream where they are carried to the cells in your body.

Carbohydrates

Marathon runners fuel up on big pasta dinners before they race. That's because our body gets most of its energy from carbohydrates found in bread, pasta, rice, and other starches.

Protein

The amino acids in protein build, repair, and help maintain all the cells in your body. Meat, fish, and poultry are good sources of protein. So are eggs, beans, and nuts.

Fats

Besides supplying energy, fats make up an important part of many cells. Your body draws on these fats when food is scarce. Fat also insulates your body and helps keep you warm. Not all fats are good for you. Saturated fats, found in butter and meat, should be kept to a minimum, and stay away from trans fats that are found in processed foods. Mono-unsaturated fats, such as olive oil, are a healthy choice.

Vitamins and Minerals

Your body doesn't need large amounts of most vitamins and minerals. But they are necessary to keep your body working in top shape. Calcium, found in milk products, is a mineral your body needs to make sure your teeth and bones stay healthy. Carrots, sweet potatoes, and leafy green vegetables are rich in vitamin A, which is necessary for good eyesight.

Water

Your body could last weeks without food, but not without water. Water is found in every cell and tissue in your body. It carries nutrients to cells and gets rid of waste products.

SUPERFOODS

Superfoods are packed with nutrients that may keep your immune system strong and help you stay healthy. They are foods that many people include in their diets as much as possible. Here are just a few:

Sweet Potatoes

One of the most nutritious vegetables around, sweet potatoes contain potassium, vitamins C and A, calcium, and iron.

Whole Grains

Whole grains such as oatmeal, brown rice, and quinoa are a great source of minerals, carbohydrates, vitamins B and E, and a healthy dose of fiber.

Yogurt

Yogurt has calcium, protein, carbohydrates, and vitamin B. The kind that contains live active cultures is good for digestion.

Blueberries

Besides being tasty and low in calories, blueberries are rich in antioxidants—nutrients that may help prevent certain diseases.

Eggs

A good source of protein, eggs provide you with more than a dozen vitamins and minerals.

WHAT Is the Difference Between Omnivores, Carnivores, and Herbivores?

Most humans are omnivores. So are black bears, raccoons, and pigs. But not crocodiles, snakes, or dolphins. So what's an omnivore? Someone who eats a varied diet made up of meat (including fish and poultry) and plant products. For breakfast, do you like bacon with your blueberry pancakes? Then you're an omnivore.

Meet a Meateater

House cats, like all members of the feline family, are carnivores. They eat an all-meat diet, although they may occasionally nibble on grass to help settle their stomachs. Other carnivores include sharks, wolves, polar bears, owls, and other birds of prey. Even some plants are carnivorous. The Venus flytrap digests insects and spiders that get caught in its leaves.

Grazers

Then there are herbivores, animals that eat only plant products. Horses, zebras, elephants, and deer survive mainly on grasses. Cows and some other herbivores have multiple stomachs that help them digest the bulky plant material.

The Whole Tooth

Looking at the teeth of an animal can often tell you if it's an omnivore, carnivore, or herbivore. A carnivore has mostly long, sharp teeth for tearing flesh. An herbivore has large, flat molars for crushing and grinding plants. An omnivore has both sharp front teeth and flat back molars.

From TIME FOR KIDS

A Cat's Teeth

CANINES are pointy and sharp. They stab and tear food.

INCISORS are sharp but flat. They bite and cut food.

MOLARS are wide and strong. They crush and mash up food.

VEGETARIANS

Tofu salad with vegetables

Although humans as a species are omnviores, many people prefer to avoid eating meat. Vegetarians are people who eat fruits, vegetables, grains, eggs, and dairy products. Vegans, on the other hand, only eat plant products.

If you are vegetarian, it's important to get enough protein. One way is to replace meat with beans, soy products such as tofu, and dairy products.

WHAT Is Gelatin Made From?

From the marshmallow floating on top of your mug of hot chocolate to gummy candy to the jiggly green dessert in the school cafeteria, gelatin is used in many foods. But what exactly is it made from? Gelatin is a product that comes from animals. It's made by soaking the bones and skins from cows or pigs in large vats of an acidic solution. The bones and skins are rich in collagen, a protein.

After the bones and skins soak, they are boiled in distilled water, then the solids are strained from the liquid and left to dry. The dried remains are ground into a tasteless powder called gelatin.

When the powder is stirred into hot water and then chilled, an amazing transformation takes place. It becomes a jelly-like substance that is not exactly a solid, but not a liquid either. So what is it? Gelatin is a colloid, a substance that has properties of both a liquid and a solid.

Pure protein, gelatin is easy to digest. It's a great thickener and you can find it in some yogurts, soups, and salad dressings.

Other Uses

Gelatin isn't just used in food. It's also used:
- As a thickener in shampoos and hair conditioners
- As a coating for medicine tablets, caplets, and capsules
- As a shell for paintballs

WHAT'S More . . .

People who don't eat animal products won't eat foods that contain gelatin. Instead they substitute it with agar, a vegetable protein that works much like gelatin.

This Japanese dessert was made with red bean jelly and agar.

TRY IT!

Make Smoothie POPS

Makes eight to 12 pops

Because of the gelatin, these pops won't drip as you eat them. Make sure an adult helps you with this recipe.

What You Need

- 1 box flavored gelatin, such as strawberry or orange
- 2 cups very hot water
- 2 cups vanilla yogurt, room temperature
- Ice-pop molds or small paper cups and pop sticks

What to Do:

1. Put the gelatin in the hot water and stir until the gelatin has completely dissolved.

2. Mix in the yogurt.

3. Pour the mixture into ice pop molds. If you are using paper cups, cover them with aluminum foil and put a pop stick into the center of each one.

4. Freeze for two hours or until firm.

WHAT Was the First Meal Eaten on the Moon?

In 1969, there were two sets of meals carried in *Apollo 11*'s lunar module—the craft that carried astronauts to the moon for the first time. Meal A consisted of bacon, peaches, sugar cookies, pineapple-grapefruit juice, and coffee. Meal B was beef stew, cream of chicken soup, fruitcake, grape punch, and an orange drink. Astronauts Neil Armstrong and Edwin "Buzz" Aldrin each ate two meals while on the moon. The first one they ate was Meal A.

Just Add Water

All the meals the astronauts ate during the *Apollo 11* mission were freeze-dried, preheated to kill bacteria, or dehydrated—all liquid was taken out of the food. When the astronauts were ready to eat, each food item was rehydrated and warmed in its own pouch, then scooped up with a spoon. Neil Armstrong's all-time favorite space meal was spaghetti with meat sauce, scalloped potatoes, fruitcake, and grape punch.

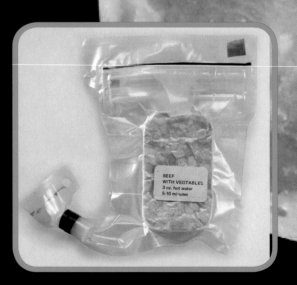

The pineapple fruitcake served on Apollo missions could be eaten as is.

An astronaut had to add water through a nozzle in order to eat this meal of beef with vegetables.

Other Famous Food Firsts in Space

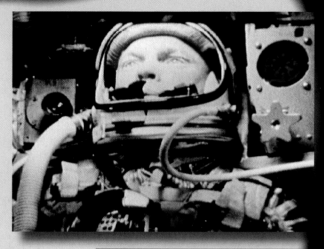

○ The first astronaut to eat in space was **John Glenn** aboard *Friendship 7* on February 20, 1962. He dined on applesauce squeezed from a tube, and nibbled on malted milk tablets.

○ The first astronaut crew to use eating utensils were the *Apollo 8* team in 1968. Before that, astronauts had to sip food through straws or eat with their hands.

○ The first corned beef sandwich in space was eaten by **Virgil Grissom** in 1965. Astronaut **John Young** smuggled the sandwich aboard the *Gemini 3* spacecraft and gave it to the mission's commander.

○ Astronaut Sandra Magnus was the first person to cook a meal in space. In 2008, aboard the International Space Staion, she whipped up a tasty meal of grilled tuna by cooking ingredients in foil packets and then heating them in a food warmer.

Astronauts John Young (left) and Virgil Grissom aboard *Gemini 3*.

WHAT'S More . . .

It seems fast food is available everywhere, even in space. In 2001, Pizza Hut sent a vacuum-sealed pizza to astronauts aboard the International Space Station.

WHAT Are Some Insects You Can Eat?

What's for dinner? How about starting with grilled scorpions on a stick, followed by barbecued grubs, and roasted tarantulas? And for dessert, you can snarf down some chocolate-covered ants. In many parts of the world, people gobble up insects and arachnids such as spiders, scorpions, and ticks. Insects are an excellent source of protein as well as vitamins and minerals. What's more, there are lots of them. Insects make up four-fifths of all the species on Earth. Who knows? One day, the old saying "butterflies in your stomach" may become more than just an expression.

Crunchy Crickets

Crickets, besides being packed with protein, are high in calcium. With a nutty, crunchy taste, crickets can be a problem to eat whole as their legs, wings, and antennae often get stuck between teeth or, more dangerously, in the throat. That's why many cricket crunchers grind them into a fine powder.

Witchetty Grubs

If you like almonds, then you may like the taste of witchetty grubs, jumbo-size larvae from moths that feed on the roots of witchetty bushes. Native Australians have eaten the grubs for thousands of years. They are traditionally enjoyed raw, but when they are cooked, the skin crisps up, leaving the delicate flesh inside creamy and tender.

Stink Bugs

In the United States, stink bugs are pests that devour crops, but in Mexico and in parts of Africa, they are enjoyed in stews and sauces. The bugs give off a stinky liquid when they are disturbed, so they have to be handled with care. In Africa, people place the bugs in warm water and stir them until the bugs release their liquid. After several rinses, they are ready to be boiled. In Mexico, one type of stink bug has a spicy cinnamon flavor that comes from the plants it feeds on. Rich in vitamin B, the tiny bugs are added to sauces and used as a filling for tacos.

Fried Tarantulas

Imagine coming home from school to munch on a snack of fried tarantula. Many kids in Cambodia, a nation in Asia, do just that. The spiders are dusted with salt, sugar, and seasoning and then fried in oil and garlic. The size of an adult's palm, a protein-packed tarantula is eaten whole, although it's okay to pull off the crunchy legs and nibble them first. Save the gooey abdomen for last.

A Mouthful of Mealworms

About an inch long, mealworms, the larvae of the darkling beetle, are found throughout the world. They taste like whatever food they've been raised on. So, if a mealworm fed on corn flour, it would taste like corn. If it feasted on wheat flour, it would have a doughy taste.

WHAT'S More...

Insects are arthropods, animals with a hard outer skeleton and limbs with joints so they can bend. Shellfish such as shrimp and crabs are also arthropods.

WHAT Is an Ackee?

An ackee is a tropical fruit that is originally from West Africa and brought by slaves to the islands of the Caribbean. People who like ackee know they have to be very careful when they boil and eat it or they will get very sick. The only edible part is the ripe yellow flesh. An ackee's buttery-nutty flavor is delicious and tastes a lot like scrambled eggs. The fruit is rich in fatty acids, protein, vitamin A, and zinc.

If the flesh is eaten before the ackee matures, though, it's poisonous. So are the fruit's large black seeds, which should never be eaten. Even the water in which the ackee is boiled is dangerous to drink.

WHAT'S More...

The ackee is the national fruit of Jamaica, an island-nation in the Caribbean. Ackee and codfish is the country's national dish. Jamaicans know how to cook the fruit so it's safe to eat.

More DANGEROUS Foods

Cassava

You might not know the cassava plant, but there is a good chance you've tasted tapioca pudding, whose main ingredient is produced by the cassava's roots. The cassava plant can be deadly, though, if the roots and leaves are served raw. That's because the plant contains cyanide, a poison.

Puffer Fish

The puffer fish is a tasty delicacy in Japan and is served in wafer-thin slices. However, its intestines and liver contain a deadly poison that could kill 30 people. Good thing a chef trains for as long as three years before becoming licensed to prepare the fish.

Mushrooms

There are many kinds of mushrooms in the world, and the ones you buy in food stores are good for you. But many types of mushrooms are poisonous. Unless you are a mycologist (a mushroom expert), you should never pick or eat a mushroom you find in the woods—no matter how pretty it is.

Stay away! Poison!

WHAT Are the Ingredients in Chewing Gum?

The main ingredient in chewing gum is a gum base. That's what makes it so chewy. Most gum bases today are made from manmade rubber, and are indigestible, which means they won't break down in your body.

Softeners such as glycerin are added to the gum base to keep the base moist and to prevent the gum from hardening. Bubble gum is just regular chewing gum that contains more of the base and the softener. Sweeteners, usually sugar or corn syrup, come next. The last ingredient added is the flavoring. The most popular flavors are spearmint, peppermint, and cinnamon.

Non-sticky Gum

Ever step on a wad of gum or get some tangled in your hair? A new gum has been invented that might make the problem of sticky gum a thing of the past. Terence McCarthy, a British professor, developed a gum that disintegrates into a fine powder when mixed with water. McCarthy got his idea after visiting the United States and seeing all the hardened gum that darkened the sidewalks.

Chewing GUM Through the Ages

○ The **mastic tree** is a small tree that grows in Greece. Ancient Greeks used to chew on its resin, which dripped from the tree in liquid form and dried into hard bits. As the Greeks chewed, the resin softened and became gum. Mastic gum has a piney flavor.

○ The Mayans chomped on gum as well, using **chicle** as their gum base. The chicle tree is native to Mexico and Central America. To get at the gum, the Mayans made gashes along the trunk in a zigzag pattern and collected the drippings, which were then boiled until thickened. Until the1960s, chicle was the main ingredient in gum. Then, it was replaced with artificial gum bases.

○ American Indians from the Northeast chewed **resin from spruce trees**. They passed this habit along to the early American settlers who, by the 1800s, started selling lumps of the gum. This made spruce gum the first commercial chewing gum.

Resin

CHICLE GUM
Achras Zapota L.
Sapotaceae
Chewing gum from C. America
A675082

This preserved chicle gum is from the 1800s.

Resin is collected by having it drip into a bag.

WHAT'S More...

The world's oldest known piece of chewing gum is 5,000 years old. An archaeology student in Finland, a nation in northern Europe, discovered a hunk of tar made from birch bark. The gum had human teeth marks on it.

WHAT Is Poutine?

A basic poutine (pooh-*teen*), is a plate of French fries mixed with fresh cheese curds and then smothered with brown gravy. Poutine, which is French slang for "mess," got its start in rural Quebec, Canada, about 50 years ago. Later it spread to other parts of Canada and today is a national dish.

The key to a tasty poutine is cheese curds, the fresher the better. Curds are the solid parts of milk that have been soured during the cheese-making process. Cheese curds squeak when you bite into them. The louder the squeak, the fresher the curds.

Poutine is high in calories, fat, and salt. It definitely isn't meant to be eaten all the time. A side dish of the stuff can contain as much as 750 calories and 41 grams of fat.

WHAT'S More . . .

If you go to a Burger King or a McDonald's in Canada, you'll most likely find poutine on the menu.

Some More National Dishes

Borscht

Ukraine

Considered a meal in itself, borscht is a hearty beet soup. Some versions are so thick that a spoon can stand upright in the bowl. Borscht contains beets, but each region in the Ukraine adds something to the basic soup. For instance, in Kiev, cooks add lamb and mushrooms. Elsewhere potatoes or squash and apples might thicken the broth.

Adobo

Philippines

Filipinos cook meat in vinegar to keep it fresh in the tropical climate. So it's no surprise that their national dish is a meat stew marinated and cooked in a vinegary broth.

Haggis

Scotland

Take the heart, liver, and lungs of a sheep, cut them into tiny bits, combine that with onions, oatmeal, stock, and spices, and simmer everything in the lining from a sheep's stomach for several hours. That's haggis, a pudding that is usually served with "neeps and tatties," or mashed turnips and potatoes.

Kimchi

Korea

In Korea, kimchi, a pickled, fermented vegetable dish, is traditionally made from cabbage. It is eaten as a side dish with breakfast, lunch, and dinner.

WHAT If You Run into a Bear in the Wild?

If you are hiking or camping in bear country, let your wild neighbors know you're there. Make plenty of noise so that a bear will hear you coming and stay out of your way. Don't set up camp near hiking trails. Bears use them just like people do. Finally, food attracts bears. Keep supplies away from your campsite and hang food from a rope between two trees. Clean your site after meals. Bears are excellent sniffers and will track down leftovers, so burn any garbage. And remember: Never go hiking or camping without an adult.

If You Do Run into a Bear . . .

Stay calm and it's likely the bear will leave. Most bears attack only to protect their territory, food, or their cubs. If the bear follows, stop. Do not run. Curl up in a ball, and don't move. In most cases, the bear will leave when it no longer sees you are a threat.

Reading a Bear

A bear's body language can give you valuable clues about its mood. If the bear is swaying its head, clacking its teeth, and huffing, watch out! It is upset and likely to attack. Another sign of an angry bear is when its ears are pressed flat and its head is lowered. A bear standing on its hind legs is usually curious and just trying to get a better look or smell.

Watch Out!

What's Up?

What would you do if you came face to face with a wild animal, or were forced to go without food and water? Chances are excellent that these events won't happen, but just in case, here's how to be prepared.

WHAT If You Come Across a Snake?

Snakes are found everywhere. You might come across one in a forest, in the tropics, in the desert, or even in your backyard. Most snakes are harmless—to humans at least. But some species have glands that produce a poisonous venom that they inject to kill prey. They also use it in self-defense. If you step on a snake or walk too close to one, it will most probably strike out and attack. That's why it's important to follow these safety rules.

- Don't pick up or touch any snake unless you are 100 percent sure it isn't venomous.

- Wear boots and long pants if you are walking through tall grass or places where snakes might hide. It's also a good idea to carry a stick and pound the ground with it to let snakes know you're passing through.

- Don't place your hands in cracks in stone walls or logs without first checking them for snakes.

- Set up your campsite in a clearing, far away from trees, grass, and boulders.

Snakes to Avoid

Eastern Diamondback Rattlesnake
North America's most dangerous snake, this rattlesnake can reach 96 inches. You'll find it in the southeastern United States.

Cottonmouth
These aggressive snakes are often spotted sunning themselves near water. They are found in the southeastern United States.

Coral Snake
With their bright bands of red, yellow, and black, coral snakes are easy to identify. You'll find them in the lower southern states, as well as in Arizona and New Mexico.

Sidewinder
Although their venom is not as toxic as some other snakes, sidewinders are dangerous and a bite from one will hurt—a lot. These super-fast snakes live in the sandy deserts of the southwestern United States.

WHAT If You Get Lost While Hiking?

No one likes to get lost, especially when you're in the wilderness. That's why it is important to go hiking with a grown-up and to always let someone know where you are and what time to expect you back. Sometimes, though, even the best plans go wrong and you lose your way. Follow these tips, and you'll be out of the woods in no time.

Stay Put. Once you realize you're lost, the number one rule is to stay put. Don't wander about. You'll only make it harder for people to find you.

Take Cover. If it's cool, stay as warm and as dry as possible. If it's hot, you'll need to cool off. Stay in the shade and don't move around.

Make Noise. Make it easy for people to find you. Carry a whistle and a bright bandana so you can be more easily seen and heard. Wave your bandana and blow your whistle three times every few minutes. If you don't have a bandana or a whistle, alternately wave your hands and pound two rocks together.

Take a Snack. Always take a snack and water with you. Don't eat any food you find growing in the wild.

Your Outdoor Survival Kit

hat

compass

whistle

bandana

GPS

flashlight

extra batteries

snacks

water

WHAT Is the Lowest Body Temperature a Person Has Survived?

Anna Bagenholm, a Swedish doctor, went skiing one winter day in 1999, never imagining she'd end up in medical textbooks. While skiing, Bagenholm tumbled into an icy stream and became trapped under a thick layer of ice. With her head and upper body in freezing water, she found an air pocket and managed to hang on for the 80 minutes it took for rescue workers to free her. By the time she reached a hospital, she had no heartbeat and her temperature was 56.7 degrees Fahrenheit—about 42 degrees lower than normal. The doctor didn't think she would live.

Bagenholm was found in the mountains near the town of Narvik, Norway.

Luckily, Bagenholm did live because her body cooled way down before her heart stopped. With a much slower metabolism, her cells didn't need as much oxygen. She holds the record for being the only person to survive such a low body temperature. Today, Bagenholm is once again working— and skiing.

When Is HOT, TOO HOT?

As temperatures climb higher and the humidity rises, your body has to work harder to cool down. Sometimes, though, a body makes or takes in too much heat and can't cool down quickly enough. If the body's temperature goes above 105 degrees Fahrenheit, a condition known as heat stroke occurs. Symptoms include hot, dry skin, a rapid pulse, headache, and vomiting. Sweating, the body's natural cooling system, stops completely.

The best way to get over heat stroke is to find a place with air conditioning and bathe in cool water. If you are out in nature, find shade and use water to cool off.

WHAT Is the Longest a Person Can Survive Without Water?

If you've ever played a sport in really hot weather, you know how quickly you lose water through sweating. The human body also loses water through urine and poop. This water must be replaced. Water regulates our body temperature, flushes out waste products, and helps carry nutrients and oxygen to our cells. That's why doctors recommend that people drink at least eight cups of water a day. If you are very active or if the weather is very hot, you need to drink more.

So how long can people survive without water? If they are healthy adults and the weather is mild, humans can go without water for three to eight days. Under extreme conditions, when temperatures are high, a person might survive two days.

Dehydration

When people don't have enough water in their bodies, they become dehydrated. At first the signs are mild. Your body won't produce as much saliva and urine. If dehydration continues, your mouth becomes dry and your heart beats faster. With severe dehydration, your body produces no urine at all.

What is the longest a person can survive without food?

While no one can last long without H_2O, a healthy person can go up to two months without eating. The human body stores energy in the form of fat, so the chunkier a person is, the longer he or she will survive. As the stores of fat are depleted, the body starts to get weaker.

Don't Try This At Home!

David Blaine, the magician, went 44 days in 2003 without a bite to eat. And he did so suspended inside a clear plastic box dangling over the Thames River in England (photo, right). When his stunt ended, he had lost 54 pounds.

David Blaine waits to leave his box after going without food for 44 days. He did drink plenty of water, however.

WHAT Is the Deepest a Person Has Dived?

One of the world's most extreme and dangerous sports, free diving is an activity in which competitors take a single breath before diving underwater. There are different types of free-dive competitions, some taking place in pools and others in the ocean. Of all of them, No-Limit is the one that lets a diver go the deepest.

In No-Limit, a diver rides a weighted "sled" down to the ocean's depths. In 2007, Austrian Herbert Nitsch set the record for the deepest free dive. On his sled, Nitsch dove an amazing 702 feet—the length of a 70-story building—in ocean waters. He completed the dive on one gulp of air, holding his breath for more than four minutes.

How Do They Do It?

What makes it possible for a human to dive so deep? It's something that all warm-blooded creatures share, called the mammalian diving reflex. The response is triggered once the face is submerged in cold water. First, the heartbeat slows. As the body dives deeper, the pressure of all that water makes the blood in the limbs withdraw, forcing it into the chest and to vital organs, such as the heart. As this takes place, the lungs become smaller and smaller until they are the size of lemons. The shrunken lungs can now work on less oxygen.

Herbert Nitsch is pulled out of the water after diving 342 feet at a competition in 2005.

And the Winner for Deepest Animal Diver Is...

Don't hold your breath! The **sperm whale** has the honor of deepest air-breathing animal, diving to depths of 6,500 feet. Runners up include the Cuvier's beaked whale at 6,200 feet, the elephant seal at 5,000 feet, and the leatherback turtle at 4,200 feet.

Strolling on the Ocean Floor

Marine biologist Sylvia Earle set a world record in 1979 when, after descending 1,250 feet in a tiny submarine, she left the underwater vehicle and walked across the ocean floor. Earle, wearing a special pressurized diving suit and breathing through an oxygen tank, walked on the sea bottom for more than two hours, marveling at the strange creatures she saw there.

Sylvia Earle explores the ocean's depths.

WHAT Is the Longest a Person Can Survive in Space Without Protection?

Outer space holds many dangers. It has extreme temperatures, from highs of more than 200 degrees Fahrenheit to lows of -380 degrees Fahrenheit. Then there's deadly radiation from cosmic rays and hurling particles of space dust. But if an astronaut were to step outside a spacecraft without any protection, none of this would really matter. Since space is a vacuum, without oxygen and air pressure, no one could survive for even two minutes.

Astronaut Franklin R. Chang-Díaz, wearing an EMU, works on the International Space Station.

A One-Man Spacecraft

And that's why astronauts wear space suits when they need to leave their craft. These extravehicular mobility units (EMUs) protect astronauts from the dangers of space and allow them to go on space walks to make repairs, or to help build the International Space Station. A space suit provides air pressure. It does this by surrounding the body with air held in by rubberized fabric. In a way, an astronaut is inside a giant balloon.

Astronauts also carry on their backs a life support system that provides them with pure oxygen. To protect astronauts from the extreme temperatures of space, EMU designers use insulated layers of fabric. The outer layer reflects sunlight. The fabric is extra tough to prevent rips from tiny specks of meteoroids whizzing past at high speeds.

A space suit is made up of many layers, 13 in all, from the undergarments that keep an astronaut cool to the outer assembly, helmet, gloves, and life support system. Astronauts mix and match the pieces for a custom fit.

WHAT'S More . . .

The space suit Neil Armstrong wore to walk on the moon in 1969 weighed 200 pounds on Earth. Today's modern space suit weighs even more. The backpack alone is more than 300 pounds. Designers are working on creating space suits that will weigh much less.

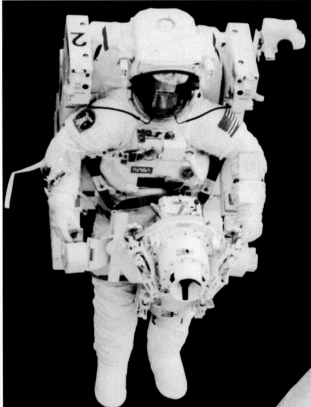

Free Flying

Astronauts in early EMU space suits needed to be tethered, or tied, to the mother ship with 25-foot-long cords, hampering their movements. It wasn't until 1984 that astronaut **Bruce McCandless** became the first person to go on a space walk tether-free. He zipped around wearing a Manned Maneuvering Unit (MMU) jet pack.

WHAT Is a Perfect Game in Baseball?

A perfect game is every pitcher's dream—to face 27 batters and not let any of them get as far as first base. That means no runs, walks, or errors during the entire game which must last a full nine innings. A perfect game is such a rare event that from 1880-2011, only 20 pitchers in major league baseball had achieved it.

A pitcher can also shine by throwing a shutout (no runs scored against him) or a no-hitter (no hits against him). In a no-hitter, the pitcher can give up walks and errors. Although it's rare, a pitcher can pitch a no-hitter and his team can still lose. This happened to Ken Johnson of the Houston Colt .45s in 1964. (The team changed its name to the Houston Astros in 1965.) Johnson pitched nine innings against the Cincinnati Reds and didn't allow any hits. His team lost by one run, the result of an error.

WHAT'S More . . .

The only player to pitch a perfect game in the World Series was Don Larsen in 1956. In Game 5 of the series, Larsen, of the New York Yankees, faced down the Brooklyn Dodgers' 27 batters, striking out seven of them. The Yankees went on to win the series.

New York Yankees catcher Yogi Berra leaps into the arms of Yankee pitcher Don Larsen after winning the 1956 World Series.

Do you know what an alley-oop is? A musher? If someone asked you if you've ever zorbed, would you know what to say? The answers to those questions—and many more—are right here in this chapter. So, start reading. Mush!

Perfect Records

Here are the 20 pitchers who made baseball history by pitching perfect games.

PITCHER	YEAR	WINNING TEAM
Lee Richmond	1880	Worcester
Monte Ward	1880	Providence
Cy Young	1904	Boston
Addie Joss	1908	Cleveland
Charlie Robertson	1922	Chicago
Don Larsen	1956	New York
Jim Bunning	1964	Philadelphia
Sandy Koufax	1965	Los Angeles
Catfish Hunter	1968	Oakland
Len Barker	1981	Cleveland
Mike Witt	1984	California
Tom Browning	1988	Cincinnati
Dennis Martinez	1991	Montreal
Kenny Rogers	1994	Texas
David Wells	1998	New York
David Cone	1999	New York
Randy Johnson	2004	Arizona
Mark Buehrle	2009	Chicago
Dallas Braden	2010	Oakland
Roy Halladay	2010	Philadelphia

Cy Young

Dennis Martinez

Randy Johnson

Roy Halladay

WHAT Is the World's Most Popular Sport?

You'll get a kick out of this answer! It's soccer—a team sport played in almost every country in the world. More than 3 billion people either play or watch soccer, which is called football everywhere outside the United States. Soccer wasn't very popular in the U.S. until the 1970s. Immigrants to America brought the sport with them and it caught on big time.

Pele (above, left) played in the 1970 World Cup in Mexico.

Soccer Greats

Voted both Soccer Player of the 20th Century and Athlete of the 20th Century, Pele is the sport's top scorer of all time with more than 1,200 goals. A native of Brazil, Pele retired from soccer in 1977 after playing in a total of 1,363 games.

The U.S. women's Olympic soccer team, led by Mia Hamm, won gold medals in 1996 and 2004. Considered the best female soccer player in the sport's history, Hamm has scored more goals than any other female soccer player. Not only that, she's scored 158 goals playing against international teams, more than anyone in the history of the sport. (Pele scored 77 international goals.)

Mia Hamm

WHAT Is an Alley-oop?

An exciting basketball play, the alley-oop requires two players working together to score a basket. Player A looks for an opportunity and passes the ball to Player B, who jumps up, catches it in mid-air, and dunks it into the basket. Like the slam dunk, the alley-oop is impressive to watch. Many half-time shows feature both these amazing plays to thrill the fans.

One of basketball's most exciting alley-oops helped the Los Angeles Lakers beat the Portland Trail Blazers in a game in 2000. After trailing for the first three quarters, the Lakers were finally winning and wanted to stay in the lead. Kobe Bryant dribbled the ball, jumped, and passed it to Shaquille O'Neal. O'Neal leaped into the air and caught the ball with one hand, and with 40 seconds left on the clock, slammed the ball into the basket. The Lakers won the game, 89-84, and went on to win the NBA championship that year.

WHAT'S More . . .

Alley-oop comes from the French *allez-oup* (ah-laze-oop), the words a French acrobat says right before making a daring jump or leap. It may have originally meant "to go up."

Shaquille O'Neal gets ready to score a slam dunk against the Trail Blazers in Game 7 of the 2000 Western Conference Finals.

WHAT Is Lacrosse?

Lacrosse is a centuries-old sport that is a combination of football, basketball, hockey, and soccer. The game is played between two teams on a rectangular field with a goal at each end. Players score by getting a small rubber ball into their team's goal. They do this by scooping, carrying, and throwing the ball with the netted stick. Except for the goalie, no one is allowed to touch the ball. The team with the most goals at the end of the game wins.

In lacrosse, a player's size doesn't matter all that much. Speed and agility do. Players must be fast and have endurance.

Men's lacrosse has 10 players per team, and the game lasts for four periods, each one 25 minutes long. Games can be intense, with a lot of rough body contact which is why men wear protective gear. In women's lacrosse, there are 12 players on each team and the game is half as long. Body contact is not allowed.

In men's lacrosse, protective gear includes a helmet, face guard, and heavy-duty gloves.

Female lacrosse players don't need protective gear because body contact is not allowed.

North America's Oldest Sport

In the 1630s, European settlers watched Native American tribes play baggataway—a game that uses long sticks and a ball. It was a brutal sport, meant to toughen up its players so they'd become fierce warriors. The field was huge, from 1 to 1.5 miles long. Players numbered anywhere from 100 to 1,000 men. The game could last for days, as players rushed after the ball, flinging it to team members.

Settlers adapted the action-packed sport, called it lacrosse, and started playing it themselves. In 1857, George Beers of Montreal, Quebec, developed rules for the game. In 1882, the first lacrosse league was formed in the United States.

This drawing shows Native Americans playing baggataway, an early form of lacrosse, on a frozen lake.

WHAT'S More...

The French living in Canada renamed the sport lacrosse after the religious staff used by bishops, called la croix.

WHAT Is the World's Longest Dog Sled Race?

Dashing through the snow in a 12-dog open sled… It isn't likely that people who take part in the Iditarod, a grueling sled dog race, would have time to sing that version of *Jingle Bells*. They are too busy driving their dog teams over 1,049 miles of snow and ice in Alaska.

There are two trails, one used in even-numbered years, the other in odd-numbered years. Both start in Anchorage and both end in Nome. On the first Saturday in March, each driver, called a musher, stands at the rear of the sled behind the hitched pairs of dogs. At the signal, more than 50 mushers and their dog teams start the race.

Mushing to the Finish Line

For the next two weeks, humans and animals will face harsh conditions, including below-freezing temperatures, biting wind, and blizzards. Along the way are checkpoints where the mushers sign in so that officials can be sure they are following the correct route and not taking shortcuts.

After days of cold and ice and snow, the first musher enters Nome driving the sled toward the finish line, which is a wooden arch. A lantern hanging on the arch stays lit until the last musher glides through as thousands of fans cheer.

The sleds are pulled by 12 to 16 dogs. Animal doctors monitor the dogs' health during the race.

Mushers leave one of the checkpoints along the route.

ALASKA

Nome

NORTHERN TRAIL

SOUTHERN TRAIL

Anchorage

An arch with the words "End of Iditarod Dog Race" welcomes the mushers at the finish line.

WHAT Is the Tour de France?

The Tour de France is a three-week long, 2,174-mile sprint through France and some neighboring countries. Every July, the best riders from around the world gather to furiously pedal up and down mountains, and sprint along flat surfaces as they head to the finish line in Paris. Along the route, millions of fans cheer the athletes on.

The cyclists ride in teams of nine. Usually only one team member has a chance of winning. The rest are there to help the leader win. How do they do this? By riding in front during parts of the course to shield the leader from wind, by setting a pace for the leader to follow, and by making sure he has plenty of water and other supplies. Team members will even give up their bike to the leader, in case his breaks down.

The race is divided into stages, each lasting a day. There are 21 stages in all, nine of which take place in the mountains where biking is extra hard. The winner of the Tour de France is the rider with the fastest time overall.

Cadel Evans, winner of the 2011 Tour de France, raises his bike in a victory salute at the finish line in Paris.

There are about 200 cyclists who take part in the Tour de France.

WHAT'S More...

Maurice Garin was the winner of the first Tour de France in 1903. He was disqualified in the 1904 race because of cheating.

Great Moments in Sports

The final moments of the 1989 Tour de France were nail-biting ones. The two leads, American Greg LeMond (left) and Frenchman Laurent Fignon (right), approached the last 15 miles separated by 50 seconds, with Fignon in the lead. In one of the most exciting wins in the sport's history, LeMond whittled down the time second by second. He completed the race eight seconds faster than Fignon, the narrowest tour win ever.

WHAT Is Spelunking?

Some people put on snorkeling equipment and swim around ocean reefs. Other people suit up and climb to the tops of mountains. But spelunkers slap on helmets and venture deep into the Earth. Spelunking is the exploration of underground caves.

Why would people plunge thousands of feet underground into a world of strange shapes and total darkness? According to author James Tabor who wrote a book about caving, it's the challenge.

"There are some people who, when they look at a high mountain or a deep ocean or a bizarre cave, something really deep, deep, deep in them says, 'I've got to go there.' It's almost an irresistible impulse," Tabor explains.

An Awesome Journey

Spelunkers face dangers including the possibility of drowning in underground lakes and rivers, being hit with poison gases, or being buried under rockfalls. That's one reason why spelunkers explore in groups. For them the payoff is well worth the risk. Coming across strange and colorful rock formations, going where no one else has gone before, and spotting cave-dwelling creatures make the experience an under-this-world adventure.

A spelunker climbs up a rope to exit a cave in British Columbia, Canada.

Light from aboveground shines through cracks in the Earth, providing light for spelunkers.

WHAT'S
More . . .

Many people call their sport caving and prefer to be known as cavers. In the United Kingdom, the sport is called potholing.

Safety Rocks!

Thinking of exploring a cave? Here are some common sense rules:

- Always go spelunking with a grown-up. Never enter a cave alone.
- Make sure someone aboveground knows where you are at all times.
- Wear a helmet and carry a flashlight.
- Obey the spelunker's motto: Take nothing but pictures. Leave nothing but footprints. Kill nothing but time.

Some spelunkers swim in underwater caves. The man wearing a scuba-diving outfit is searching for a passage that leads to water.

WHAT Is Zorbing?

If you've ever seen a hamster running inside a clear ball, you have some idea of what zorbing is all about. Only you're the hamster. In this extreme sport, you ride inside a large plastic ball down a slope.

A zorb consists of two balls, a smaller one inside a larger one, connected by ropes to keep the balls turning as a unit. The air cushion that forms between the balls protects the rider from bumps. Both balls are made of see-through plastic. So how do you get in—and out of—a zorb? There's a 2-foot-long opening for a rider to squeeze through.

Zorbing was invented by two New Zealanders in the early 1990s. Andrew Akers and Dwayne van der Sluis wanted to create a device that would make it possible for them to walk on water. The two friends ended up with a prototype of a ball within a ball. The finished product did float, but it was impossible to steer.

Even so, the men still thought they had a great idea and decided to patent and trademark their invention. They called it the zorb. Before long, the partners hit on the bizarre idea of strapping people inside the zorb and rolling them down hills.

Are You a Dry or Wet Zorber?

There are two types of zorbing rides to choose from. For a dry ride, an operator straps you into the ball, and after making sure you're secure, releases the zorb. Down the slope you roll, head over heels, until you reach the bottom. There, another operator stops the zorb and unstraps you.

If you decide on a wet ride, you aren't strapped in. Instead the operator fills the zorb with about five gallons of water and off you go. People have compared the experience to being inside a washing machine.

WHAT Is a Pommel Horse?

This kind of horse doesn't neigh or eat hay. The pommel horse, also called a side horse, is a padded piece of gymnastics equipment. About 4 feet high and 5 feet 4 inches long, the apparatus has two handles, called pommels, that a gymnast holds onto for support when he performs routines.

The pommel horse is one of the most difficult of all gymnastic events. It requires both great skill and strength.

While performing, a gymnast must never let any part of his body—other than his hands—touch the equipment. On the pommel horse, a gymnast performs a set of moves. He swings around the horse completing circles, flairs, scissors, and handstands. At the end, he jumps off, or dismounts, landing firmly on both feet. Otherwise the judges take off points from his score.

What makes these exercises especially difficult is that the gymnast's body must be in constant motion. It is the only event in which gymnasts don't get to stop or pause during the routine.

Whoa! Daniel Purvis of Great Britain performs a scissors routine on the pommel horse.

Rings

Horse vault

More Acrobatic Apparatus

O A gymnast must have strength and great control to perform on the rings. After he's lifted onto the suspended rings, he tries to keep them as still as possible as he does handstands and other routines.

O The horse vault is a lot like the pommel horse. It's just missing the handles. Gymnasts leap off springboards and perform twists and somersaults over it.

O Two bars, 17 inches apart, make up the parallel bars. A gymnast swings and vaults from one to the other, and at some points holds completely still in order to show mastery and control.

Parallel bars

WHAT Is Motocross?

Motocross riders on their bikes seem to fly as they leap off hilltops and speed down twisty, rutted dirt roads. Motocross is a challenging type of motorcycle racing in which riders compete outdoors on a short, bumpy course made up of hills, mud tracks, and dirt roads with plenty of hair-raising turns.

Most motocross courses are one to two miles long, and up to 40 riders can compete during a race. The riders line up at the starting gate and wait for the signal to take off. The races are measured by time, usually 30 minutes. The first rider to finish the course with the most laps in the alloted time wins the race.

Riders of motocross need specialized bikes in order to take on challenging dirt courses. A motocross bike's lightweight frame and powerful motor allow it to reach high speeds and make razor sharp turns. The bike's high suspension absorbs shocks from bumpy roads, while chunky treads grip surfaces that can range from sand to rock-hard clay.

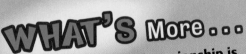

The AMA Motocross Championship is the world's top motocross race. It was first held in 1974.

In motocross, some of the jumps can be as high as 20 feet.

Similar to motocross, supercross is motorcycle racing held in indoor stadiums. The courses are shorter than motocross, usually about one-half of a mile.

Bikes compete in individual races according to their engine size. Professional riders zoom around on bikes with huge 500 cc engines. Kids ride bikes with less powerful 50 cc engines.

WHAT Is Mancala?

One of the world's oldest board games, mancala has been played throughout Africa for more than 1,200 years. The word mancala comes from Arabic and means "to move." While there are many versions of the game, each with its own name, mancala is the umbrella term that covers them all.

The different versions share the same basic rules and equipment. Two players sit across from each other with the mancala board between them. The long rectangular board has indentations, or pits, in which markers, such as seeds or pebbles, are placed. Players move their markers from pit to pit around the board, trying to capture the opponent's pieces while holding on to theirs. The winner is the player who ends up with the most markers.

Today, mancala is played throughout the world. You can even find online versions of the game. One reason for its popularity is that it can be played almost anywhere. If you don't have a board, you can dig pits in the dirt or sand and use pebbles, seeds, or shells as your markers.

Make Your Own Mancala Board

What You Need

- cardboard egg carton
- scissors
- acrylic paints and brush (optional)
- 48 dried beans, pebbles, or beads
- 2 small glass jars

What to Do

1. Carefully tear or cut the lid from the carton. Throw the lid away.

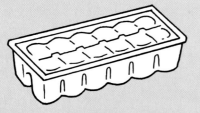

2. If you wish, paint and decorate the carton. Wait for the paint to dry.

3. Place 4 beans in each of the 12 cups. Place a jar at either end of the carton. Called a kalaha, it is where you will store any captured beans. Find a friend and get ready to play.

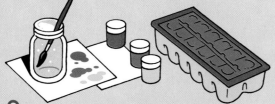

How to Play

Object of the Game: To finish with the most beans

1. Set the mancala board on a table so that six cups face you and six cups face your opponent. The cups nearest to you are yours. You can move any of the beans from your side, but you may not move your opponent's. The kalaha on your right is yours as well.

2. Flip a coin to see who goes first. Player A scoops all the beans from any one of the cups on her side. Moving counterclockwise to the right, she goes down the board, dropping one bean into each cup. If she reaches her kalaha, she drops a bean in it as well. If it's her last bean, she gets another turn. Otherwise, it's Player B's turn.

3. Play continues with the following rules:

- A player cannot drop a bean into the opposing player's kalaha.

- When the last bean a player drops falls into an empty cup, that player gets to take that bean and all the beans from the cup directly opposite.

4. The game ends when a player runs out of beans in the cups on her side. When this happens, the opposing player takes the remaining beans. The winner is the player with the most beans in her kalaha.

WHAT Is Skara Brae?

In 1850, a powerful storm pounded the Orkney Isles off the coast of Scotland, stripping grass and dirt off a huge mound. When the storm cleared, amazed islanders discovered the outlines of stone buildings buried in the mound. Over the next 80 years, archaeologists uncovered a prehistoric village, built by people who lived more than 4,500 years ago. The name of that village is Skara Brae (*scar*-ah bray) and it is older than the pyramids in Egypt.

The settlement is made up of eight buildings that are linked together by passageways. The builders buried the stonewalls in the soil with only the roofs aboveground. Snug underground, the villagers were protected from wind and cold.

Today, visitors can walk around Skara Brae and go inside the buildings.

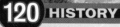

Seven of the buildings were houses, all with the same basic design. Each is made up of a square room with a fireplace in its center. On opposite sides of the room are stone beds. Across from the doorway stands a stone dresser with shelves. Sunken into the floor of each home is a tank. This was probably used to hold fish bait.

The eighth building was probably used as a workshop. The ancient villagers were skilled craftsmen, and it's likely this is where they made their stone tools. The villagers, who lived in Skara Brae from around 3100 to 2450 B.C., were farmers. They grew grain and kept cows and sheep, yet also found time to hunt and fish.

Dresser Fireplace Bed Tank Bed

WHAT'S More...

Because the only wood on the island came from driftwood, the villagers made their furniture out of stone.

Stone passageways connect the houses of Skara Brae. They allowed the villagers to travel from one building to another without having to go outside.

WHAT Did the Tuskegee Airmen Do?

During World War II, while Americans fought Hitler's racism abroad, segregation was in full swing at home. The military, like much of the United States, prevented African Americans from mixing with whites. Black soldiers lived in special units and were not allowed to do certain jobs, such as fly planes. Although qualified pilots were badly needed, the military rejected black applicants, believing that they weren't physically or mentally fit to fly planes.

After much pressure, in 1939, Congress approved the Civilian Pilot Training Program (CPTP). The program taught civilians how to fly. In 1941, an all-black base in Tuskegee, Alabama, started preparing African Americans to become fighter pilots. Military leaders, however, did not expect African Americans to succeed.

When First Lady Eleanor Roosevelt visited the Tuskegee Army Air Field, she insisted on flying in an airplane with a black pilot. A strong supporter of equality, Mrs. Roosevelt used a photo of her taken with the pilot to convince the President to allow the airmen to do more than just train for battle. They should be allowed to fight in the war.

Pilot C. Alfred "Chief" Anderson takes First Lady Eleanor Roosevelt on a spin.

Members of the 332 Fighter Group pose in front of a P-51 plane.

By 1944, four all-black squadrons joined together to form the 332nd Fighter Group, known as the Red Tails. The pilots flew P-51 Mustang fighter planes that escorted U.S. bombers in raids over Italy and North Africa. They flew more than 15,000 mission flights and took down 261 enemy planes.

In spite of all their achievements, the Red Tails served their country in segregated bases at home and abroad. It wasn't until 1948, after World War II was over, that President Harry Truman signed an order that desegregated the armed forces.

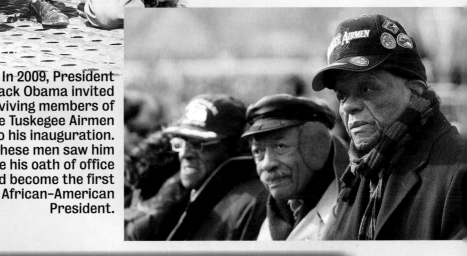

In 2009, President Barack Obama invited surviving members of the Tuskegee Airmen to his inauguration. These men saw him take his oath of office and become the first African-American President.

Bessie Coleman: Trailblaizer

Bessie Coleman was the first African American to get her pilot's license, and in order to do so she had to train in France. Coleman, who received her license in 1922, died four years later in an airplane accident. Her efforts inspired other African Americans to learn to fly and paved the way for the success of the Tuskegee Airmen.

WHAT Was the First Natural History Museum in the U.S.?

Charles Willson Peale had an exciting life. He was a captain in the Revolutionary War (1775-1781) and an artist. He painted portraits of many of the founding fathers, including George Washington, Thomas Jefferson, and Benjamin Franklin. He displayed many of his works in his Philadelphia home, naming the room the "Gallery of Great Men." It was America's first art gallery.

Peale was also deeply interested in science and nature. He collected "natural curiosities" that he also displayed, such as fossils. In 1786, when his home became too small to hold his collection, Peale moved it to another building which became the first public natural history museum in the country.

Incredible Collections

The collection grew. By 1805 the museum had 90 mammals, 700 birds, and 4,000 insects. Peale added artifacts and natural history specimens he discovered, and friends donated their finds as well. Thomas Jefferson gave the museum many of its fossils. In order to preserve the specimens he received, Peale learned taxidermy. Not all of the animals at the museum were stuffed, however. Visitors also got to see live animals, including a bald eagle and a grizzly bear.

Peale painted this self-portrait in 1822. He is pulling back the curtain to his museum.

Big Bones

On Christmas Eve in 1801, Charles Peale unveiled his latest exhibit—the complete skeleton of a mastodon, a large, hairy, prehistoric animal related to today's elephant. Standing more than 11 feet high, its tusks were longer than a grown man. The mastodon was the museum's star attraction.

A mastodon's jaw and teeth

Peale and his crew dug up the bones of a mastodon and put them together. His son drew this picture of the skeleton.

A scapula
B Humerus
C Radius
D Ulna
E Tarsus
F metatarsus
G os femoris
H Patella
I Tibia
K fibula

WHAT Is Ellis Island?

From 1892-1924, more than 12 million immigrants sailed past the Statue of Liberty in New York Harbor and landed at Ellis Island. They were coming to America from all over Europe in search of a better life for themselves and their families.

At Ellis Island, doctors examined the immigrants. If they were in good health, they would be allowed to go ashore in New York City to begin their new lives. As many as 10,000 people passed through the facility each day.

In 1924, Ellis Island stopped being the main immigrant center and it closed in 1954. Today, visitors can go to the museum on Ellis Island and learn what immigrants experienced as they arrived in the United States.

WHAT'S More...

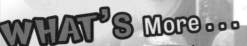

About 40 percent of all U.S. citizens have at least one ancestor who came through Ellis Island.

After doctors examined the new arrivals, the immigrants waited in the Great Hall to be interviewed by government inspectors.

Citizen Smarts

In order to become a U.S. citizen, immigrants must pass an exam that tests their knowledge of U.S. government, history, and civics. Here are some questions similar to those on the real test. Take it and see how well you do!

1. Who signs bills into laws?

2. In what year was the Constitution written?

3. Why does the flag have 13 stripes?

4. How many states are there?

5. Who has the power to declare war?

6. What is the head executive of a state government called?

7. How many times may a U.S senator be re-elected?

8. What is the national anthem of the United States?

9. What holiday was celebrated for the first time by the colonists?

10. What is the highest court in the United States?

ANSWERS: 1. The President; 2. 1787; 3. The stripes represent the original 13 colonies; 4. 50; 5. Congress; 6. The governor; 7. There is no limit. 8. "The Star-Spangled Banner"; 9. Thanksgiving; 10. The Supreme Court

Immigrants' suitcases are piled up as their owners wait to enter the U.S.

WHAT Is a Ghost Town?

Imagine you're a traveler and you've come to a town in the middle of nowhere. You're hungry and thirsty, but when you enter a restaurant no one is there to serve you. All the tables are empty. You go to a grocery store, and cans of peas and carrots sit on shelves under thick layers of dust. You wander from building to building, and don't see a soul. Finally, it hits you. You've stumbled upon a ghost town.

A ghost town is any town or city that's been abandoned by the people who lived there. What causes a community to up and leave? There are many reasons, but the most common one is if a place's resources or jobs disappear. In the western part of the United States, many towns sprang up during the California Gold Rush that began in 1848. Miners would settle a town and work nearby mines for gold. Once the gold dried up, the miners moved on, leaving the small towns they created. Today, many of these towns are tourist attractions.

Disasters, whether caused by humans or by nature, can also force people to abandon a town.

Abandoned buildings, homes, and cars make up the ghost town of Bodie, California.

Famous Ghost Towns

- People had lived in the hillside village of Craco, in southern Italy, for more than 1,000 years. Then in 1963 a landslide forced the residents to move. They never returned.

- The town of Kolmanskop was built on top of sand dunes in southern Africa's Namib Desert. Miners who worked at a nearby diamond mine lived there until the town was abandoned in the 1950s. Since then the desert has taken over the buildings, filling the homes with sand.

- Settled in 1879, more than 8,000 people once lived in Bodie, California, a gold-mining town. Today, Bodie is a California Historical State Park. Visitors can see the 150 buildings that make up the town.

Craco, Italy

Kolmanskop, Namibia

WHAT Was the Jazz Age?

For Americans, the 1920s were a swinging time. World War I had recently ended, and people were making more money than ever before. They bought cars, radios, and new-fangled appliances, such as refrigerators, washing machines, and vacuum cleaners. They were out to enjoy life to the fullest. People poured into movie theaters, where they watched silent movies and, starting in 1927, the first talkies. They visited dance halls, swinging their arms and knocking their knees together as they danced the Charleston. They went to clubs to hear jazz, music that combined the beats of Africa with the instruments of Europe.

This exciting period came to be known as the Jazz Age. The good times lasted until 1929, when the stock market crashed and plunged the nation into the Great Depression, a time of very high unemployment.

WHAT'S More . . .

Jazz got its start in the 1880s in New Orleans, Louisiana. Funeral bands playing brassy music would march behind hearses. By the 1920s, jazz became known throughout the United States.

SACK AMUSEMENT ENTERPRISES present

DUKE ELLINGTON
AND HIS
COTTON CLUB ORCHESTRA
in
BLACK AND TAN
with
FREDI WASHINGTON

Jazz great Duke Ellington (1899–1974) was a composer, pianist, and orchestra leader. He is shown at the piano in this photo.

The Flap Over Flappers

The 1920s brought big changes for women. Many wore shorter skirts, cut their long hair, and put on lipstick and make up. Called "flappers," they did the kind of things that once only men did, such as drive cars. Many people, especially those who were older, disapproved of flappers' dress and behavior. And in 1929, Florida even tried to prohibit people in the state from using the word!

A flapper in a short skirt and short hairdo dances with movie star Will Rogers.

The Harlem Renaissance

During the 1920s, many black artists, poets, writers, and musicians moved to Harlem, a section of New York City, where they became known for their writing, art, and music. Today, this period in history is called the Harlem Renaissance (ren-ah-sanz). During this time, black artists were able to open the public's eyes about how difficult it was to be black in America. It was called a renaissance, or rebirth, because African Americans took their pain and suffering and successfully turned it into art.

Famous artists from this time included the poet Langston Hughes, world-famous entertainer Josephine Baker, blues singer Bessie Smith, and jazz artists Louis Armstrong and Billie Holiday.

Langston Hughes, poet

Bessie Smith, singer

131

CHAPTER 9 Holidays & Festivals

WHAT Is Fruitcake Toss Day?

JANUARY

WHEN: The first Saturday in January

It's January and all the big-ticket holidays have come and gone. But there's always something to look forward to—and in this case, it's **Fruitcake Toss Day**! Started in 1995, this wacky holiday lets people have some fun by tossing fruitcakes, those dense baked goods that are often given as Christmas gifts.

In Manitou Springs, Colorado, where the holiday got its start, people compete in different divisions. Some throw the cakes by hand, while others choose to hurl theirs via catapults and giant slingshots.

Fruitcake Toss Day isn't the only quirky holiday on the calendar. Here's a month-by-month look at some others.

FEBRUARY

WHEN: February 26

On **Tell a Fairy Tale Day**, share your favorite fairy tale with others. Then listen to theirs.

MARCH

WHEN: The first full week in March

Be proud of who you are! Be sure to take part in **Celebrate Your Name Day**.

HOWDY
MY NAME IS

People share many of the same reasons to celebrate, even if each culture does it in its own unique way. But there are some holidays that only some people take part in. Read on and join in the fun!

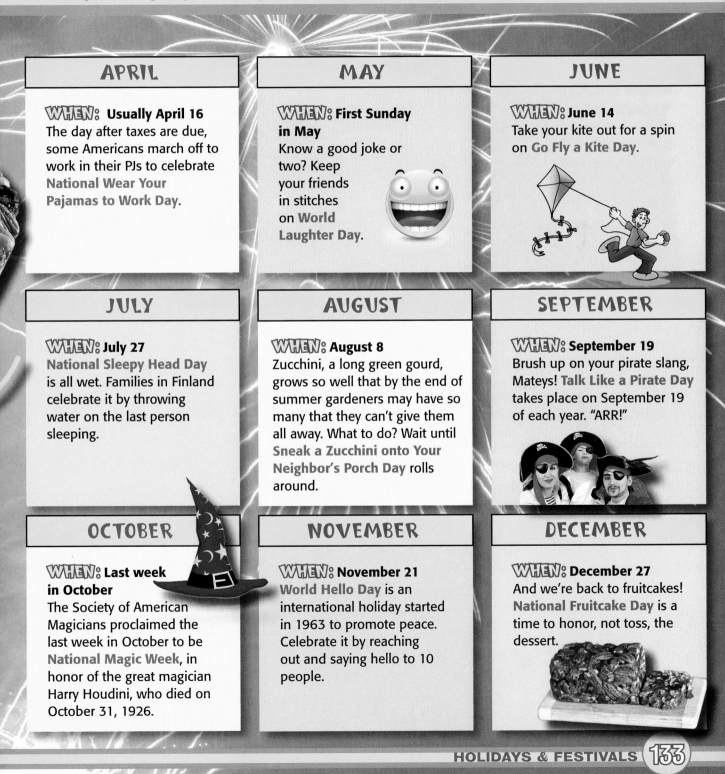

APRIL

WHEN: **Usually April 16**
The day after taxes are due, some Americans march off to work in their PJs to celebrate **National Wear Your Pajamas to Work Day.**

MAY

WHEN: **First Sunday in May**
Know a good joke or two? Keep your friends in stitches on **World Laughter Day.**

JUNE

WHEN: **June 14**
Take your kite out for a spin on **Go Fly a Kite Day.**

JULY

WHEN: **July 27**
National Sleepy Head Day is all wet. Families in Finland celebrate it by throwing water on the last person sleeping.

AUGUST

WHEN: **August 8**
Zucchini, a long green gourd, grows so well that by the end of summer gardeners may have so many that they can't give them all away. What to do? Wait until **Sneak a Zucchini onto Your Neighbor's Porch Day** rolls around.

SEPTEMBER

WHEN: **September 19**
Brush up on your pirate slang, Mateys! **Talk Like a Pirate Day** takes place on September 19 of each year. "ARR!"

OCTOBER

WHEN: **Last week in October**
The Society of American Magicians proclaimed the last week in October to be **National Magic Week**, in honor of the great magician Harry Houdini, who died on October 31, 1926.

NOVEMBER

WHEN: **November 21**
World Hello Day is an international holiday started in 1963 to promote peace. Celebrate it by reaching out and saying hello to 10 people.

DECEMBER

WHEN: **December 27**
And we're back to fruitcakes! **National Fruitcake Day** is a time to honor, not toss, the dessert.

WHAT Is Sweetest Day?

A day to celebrate candy? Not exactly. A day devoted to sweethearts? That's Valentine's Day, but you're getting closer. **Sweetest Day** is a day when we remember those among us who are less fortunate. The holiday was started in 1922 by Herbert Birch Kingston, an employee of a candy company in Cleveland, Ohio. Kingston wanted underprivileged kids to know that society hadn't forgotten them, so he organized community groups to hand out boxes of candy to the orphans and poor children in Cleveland.

Sweetest Day started out as a celebration observed in the Northeast United States. As more and more people heard about the tradition, Sweetest Day spread throughout the country. Now, many people turn the day into an opportunity to reach out to others, giving candy or small gifts to the elderly, the sick, and those in need.

Ways to Celebrate the Sweetest Day of the Year

- Become a reading or math tutor.
- Offer to rake leaves or run an errand for a neighbor.
- Send flowers to someone who is ill.
- Bake cookies and share them with your classmates.
- Design a card telling a friend why they are special to you.
- Collect clothing and toys and deliver them to a shelter.
- Start a community food drive for the needy.
- Raise money for a favorite charity.
- Put together a gift basket for a children's hospital.
- Volunteer at a senior center.

WHAT Is Ratha Yatra?

WHEN: During the Hindu Month of Asadha (End of June or Early July)

Each June, hundreds of thousands of Hindu pilgrims visit Puri (*Poor*-ee), a city on the east coast of India, to celebrate **Ratha Yatra**. The festival honors the god Jagannath (*Juhg*-uh-nawt), Lord of the Universe. Worshippers place wooden images of Jagannath, along with his sister and brother, onto three huge chariots and pull the images through Puri's streets. Brightly decorated elephants, trucks crammed with riders, and pilgrims on foot join the procession.

The chariots are pulled from one temple to another where they remain for about a week before being returned to their original home. Though Ratha Yatra festivals take place throughout India, the one in Puri is the largest.

WHAT'S More...

Each year, new chariots are built. Only wood from a certain type of tree can be used.

The chariots, called raths, look like miniature temples. Jagannath's chariot is 45 feet high and has 16 wheels, each one is seven feet in diameter. About 1,000 people pull each cart.

Pilgrims placed wooden images of the three gods inside a smaller version of the chariots.

WHAT Is Tanabata?

WHEN: July 7 or August 7

People in Japan get starry-eyed when **Tanabata** rolls around. That's because the Japanese festival celebrates the meeting of two of the brightest stars in the night sky—Vega and Altair. The date when this happens depends on where people live in Japan. Most Japanese people celebrate the festival on July 7. In some areas, though, people follow the old lunar calendar and observe Tanabata a month later.

The two stars, Vega and Altair, are tied to an ancient legend that was first told in China. According to the story, after the Sky King permits his daughter Orihime (Vega) to marry a cow herder named Hikoboshi (Altair), the two sweethearts neglect their jobs. Vega, a skilled weaver, stops weaving and Altair forgets to care for the cows. The angry king sends the couple to opposite sides of the River of Heaven (our Milky Way). He allows them to reunite only on one day of the year. When the seventh day of the seventh month arrives, a flock of magpies joins wings to create a bridge for the couple to cross.

In Hiratsuka, Japan, children walk beneath colorful paper decorations during the city's Tanabata festival.

Throughout Japan, people celebrate Tanabata by hanging colorful strips of paper on leafy bamboo branches. Many write wishes on the paper.

Make Your Own Tanabata Wish

People celebrate Tanabata by hanging paper strips with wishes on them. Here's how to make wish strips.

What You Need

- sheets of brightly-colored construction paper
- scissors
- black marker
- hole punch
- 2-inch pieces of string or yarn
- dowel or long stick

What to Do

1. Cut the construction paper in half, the long way. On each half sheet, write a wish. Encourage your family and friends to write down their wishes, too.

2. Punch a hole at the top of the sheets of paper.

3. Using string or yarn, tie your wishes to a dowel or a long stick. Display it where all can see. You can also tie your wishes to an outdoor tree branch, but be sure to get permission first.

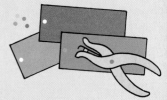

My very own dog

A long and happy life

Do well in school

An A in math

Good health

WHAT Is Holi?

WHEN: During the Hindu Month of Phalguna (February–March)

Holi is called the Festival of Colors with good reason. Observed by Hindus in India, this messy and joyous festival welcomes spring with an explosion of color. People throw paint and powder in a rainbow of hues at one another. They soak each other with colored water shot from blowpipes and water pistols. Men and women, young and old, rich and poor, mingle with one another in the streets.

The festival is held at the start of spring, usually sometime in March. In most places the festival lasts two days. In certain villages, though, the celebrations go on for up to 16 days.

The name of the festival comes from a wicked woman in Hindu mythology. Holika, the sister of an evil king, plotted with her brother to kill the king's son, Prahlad. Holika tried to burn the young prince, a devoted follower of the Hindu god Krishna. Instead, with Krishna's help, the flames consumed Holika, while Prahlad remained unharmed. The night before Holi, people light bonfires to honor this victory of good over evil.

Another story explains why people spray each other with color. According to the tale, the monkey god Hanuman swallowed the sun and cast the world in darkness. The people didn't know what to do, so the other gods suggested that the humans cover themselves with paint and squirt each other with colored water. The people obeyed. Seeing the people's antics, Hanuman started laughing, and out popped the sun.

A cloud of colored powder is tossed into the crowd.

A market in India sells powdered paint in a rainbow of colors.

Women smear colored powder on each other's faces during the celebration of Holi.

WHAT'S More . . .

Holi is celebrated in countries where there are large Hindu populations, such as Malaysia, Trinidad, and the United States.

WHAT Is Soyal?

The winter solstice is the day when Earth is farthest from the sun, which is why it is also when night is longest. On December 22, the Hopi, Native Americans living in northeastern Arizona, hold a winter solstice ceremony called a **Soyal**. The ceremony's purpose is to bring back the sun.

Many of the rituals take place in kivas (*kee*-vas), underground rooms. People enter a kiva through an opening on its top, climbing down a ladder. Before Soyal starts, priests prepare the kivas by sprinkling sacred cornmeal on the floors to purify the site. Families in the community donate ears of corn to make altars. The Hopi also make prayer sticks, which are used to bless members of the community, as well as homes, animals, and plants.

Return of the Kachinas

The Soyal is also the time when kachinas (kah-*chee*-nahs) return from their home high on the mountaintops. The Hopi believe that kachinas are spirits that protect them from harm. During Hopi ceremonies, men perform dances while dressed as kachinas.

The first kachina to make an appearance is the Soyal kachina. This kachina places prayer feathers in homes and kivas around the village, opening the way for the other kachinas to return.

Children receive carved kachina dolls as presents so they will become familiar with the different spirits.

WHAT'S More . . .

Corn, a major crop, has great importance in Hopi ceremonies. When a newborn is taken outside for the first time, he or she receives an ear of corn, a symbol of love and protection, to keep for life.

WHAT Is Mardi Gras?

Mardi Gras is a giant costume party with masks, floats, parades, and marching bands. Two of the most famous take place in New Orleans, Louisiana, and Rio de Janeiro, Brazil.

So what's the party for? It's a last hurrah before Lent, a time when Christians give up rich foods and meats to get ready for Easter. Because Lent lasts 40 days, people want to have a good time before giving up a favorite food. So for two weeks they sing, dance, and eat.

Preparations for Mardi Gras in New Orleans start early in January. People make elaborate costumes to wear and party organizers plan decorated floats for the parades. In the weeks leading up to Mardi Gras, small parades often march through neighborhoods. The most spectacular parades take place on the day before Lent. In New Orleans, huge crowds turn out to watch until, on the stroke of midnight, Mardi Gras ends.

In both New Orleans (top) and Rio de Janeiro (bottom), elaborate floats wind their way down city streets.

WHAT Is the Hungry Ghost Festival?

WHEN: 15th Day of Seventh Lunar Month (July-August)

Halloween isn't the only night when spirits come back to haunt. The **Hungry Ghost Festival** is a similar holiday, only it's observed in China and eastern Asia. According to Chinese beliefs, the seventh lunar month is known as Ghost Month, a time when the souls of the dead return from the underworld to roam among the living. The ghosts are not just beloved ancestors, but also forgotten souls who are restless and "hungry" for what people on Earth have. To calm these spirits, people burn offerings made of paper, such as fake money, houses, cars, and furniture. They also burn incense and leave food and tea for the ghosts. Some festivals feature puppet shows and performances. The first row of seats is always left empty for the ghosts.

At night, families gather at a river or stream to float homemade paper lanterns. The lanterns are shaped like the lotus flower, which is a symbol for purity and enlightenment. As the lights float downstream, people hope they will guide the spirits back to the underworld.

During Ghost Month, people float handmade paper lanterns to guide the spirits back to the underworld.

People burn fake money and other items made from paper to calm the spirits during the Hungry Ghost Festival.

Day of the Dead

On November 2, Mexicans honor their dead ancestors in a holiday called *El Dia de los Muertos* (The Day of the Dead). The holiday started as an ancient Aztec celebration of death. Today, families remember their loved ones by visiting cemeteries and decorating graves with yellow and orange marigolds. People often picnic at the gravesite, enjoying traditional foods such as *Pan de Muerto*, a sweet bread, and skulls made of sugar. At home, relatives set up shrines, placing mementos, candles, and favorite foods of the deceased inside little altars.

Decorated gravesites (top), *Pan de Muerto* (center), and sugar skulls (bottom), are all part of this ancient Mexican holiday.

CHAPTER ⑩ Mysteries

WHAT Was the Roanoke Colony?

In 1580, John White strode through the dense woods of what is now an island off the coast of North Carolina. He was headed toward the Roanoke fort, home to England's first settlement in the New World. White was governor of the small colony, and he was returning after a three-year absence.

The Mysterious Word

When he reached the fort, White was met with silence. None of the 117 colonists were there to greet him. Even the houses inside the fort had vanished. Only the posts that made up the stockade remained.

White read a word carved on one of the posts: CROATOAN. He stared at the carving in disbelief. What had happened to the colony? What had happened to his family? And what exactly, did CROATOAN mean?

White never discovered the colony's fate. The governor searched for the missing settlers and then returned to England.

In the more than 400 years since the mysterious disappearance of the Roanoke colony, historians continue to wonder what became of it. That has led to a number of theories about what might have happened.

John White depicted an Indian settlement in this watercolor.

Why Did the Colony Disappear?

Going Native

The word CROATOAN is an important clue. The Croatoan Indians were a nearby tribe that got along well with the colonists. Did the colonists leave the fort to live near or among the Indians? If the settlers were short of food and supplies, this would have made sense. But if the English did go off to live with the Croatoans, they should still be alive—and there was no trace of them.

In Enemy Hands

Perhaps a hostile Indian tribe killed the colonists. Several tribes lived in the Roanoke area and not all were friendly with the settlers. If the colony packed up and moved inland, they may have met up with one of these tribes and been captured or killed.

Starved to Death

Another idea is that the colonists died from hunger or disease. While this is a possibility, it's unlikely that every single settler would have died under these circumstances. Also, John White didn't find any gravesites at the abandoned fort.

The site of the first fort is now Fort Raleigh National Historic Site. Archaeologists look for clues about the lost colony (below).

WHAT Is the Mystery Behind Amelia Earhart's Disappearance?

Amelia Earhart was a pioneer in the sky. In 1928, she became the first woman passenger to cross the Atlantic Ocean in a plane. She was also the first female to fly solo across the U.S. without stopping. But as the world-famous pilot told reporters, "I think I have just one more long flight in my system."

So on June 1, 1937, Earhart set off from Miami, Florida, with her navigator, Fred Noonan. She was beginning her most incredible trip yet. The two were headed around the world! For the next month the pair flew to South America, and then on to Africa, Asia, and Australia. By the time the plane reached Papua New Guinea, an island north of Australia, the two had flown 22,000 miles. The next leg of their journey was the riskiest. The flyers had to head for tiny Howland Island, a speck in the vast Pacific Ocean, and more than 2,500 miles away.

On the morning of July 2, Earhart and Noonan took off for Howland Island, on what they thought would be an 18-hour flight. The plane had barely enough fuel to reach the island.

Bad Weather

As they drew nearer to Howland, the plane hit bad weather. Thick clouds and rain made it hard to navigate. Earhart and a Coast Guard radio crew were able to communicate for a while. They heard Earhart report that the weather was bad and the plane's fuel was running low. She ended her final message with the words, "We are running north and south." She was never heard from again. She and Fred Noonan vanished somewhere in the Pacific.

Amelia Earhart and Fred Noonan planned a pioneering round-the-world flight.

A huge search for the the pilot and her navigator began almost at once. But no sign of Earhart, Noonan, or wreckage of the plane was ever found.

What Happened?

In 1940, some people working on an island not far from Howland, discovered a human skull, some bones, soles from both a man and a woman's shoe, and a box used to hold navigating equipment. Did Earhart and Noonan reach this deserted island and set up camp? The evidence vanished over the years, and Earhart's disappearance continues to be an unsolved history mystery. But the pilot will always be remembered for her courage and for her pioneering role in the history of flight.

Earhart stands in front of the plane that she piloted on her ill-fated journey.

The red line shows the route that Earhart flew until her plane disappeared.

DAILY NEWS FINAL

EARHART PLANE LOST AT SEA

Amelia Earhart Missing on World Flight

WHAT Is the Oak Island Treasure Mystery?

What is buried in the Money Pit on Oak Island, Nova Scotia? The mystery has baffled treasure seekers ever since the pit was first discovered in 1795. That's when a teenage boy hunting on the uninhabited tiny island along Canada's Atlantic coast, came upon a wide depression hidden with tree branches. He'd heard tales of pirates burying treasure in the area, so he came back with two friends and they began digging. Every 10 feet down, the boys uncovered a platform of wooden logs. The hole was some sort of a shaft that had been refilled with dirt. The trio reached 30 feet down and, with no treasure in sight, had to stop.

But they didn't give up. Nine years later, they convinced a wealthy businessman to form a company to hunt for the treasure. This time they got down past 90 feet. Again, they found wooden platforms every 10 feet, as well as coconut matting and a stone carved with some kind of code. They were definitely on to something! At 93 feet, they struck something solid. Was it the treasure chest at last? They didn't find out. The next morning, the pit was two-thirds filled with water. Unable to bail out the water, the men gave up digging.

CANADA

Oak Island

WHAT'S More...

The only treasure ever found at the site was three links of a gold chain, dug up in 1849.

Workers (right and above), hoped to find the treasure of the Money Pit in 1860.

Water Traps

In 1849, another group started digging for the treasure. But the drillers had the same problems with water filling the hole. The crew figured out that the people who built the pit had installed a system of flood tunnels. Each was a trap designed to fill the hole with water to prevent the treasure from ever being found.

Today, the island is owned by businessmen hoping to finally unearth the treasure—if there is any. Will they succeed and if so, what will they find? Stay tuned.

WHAT'S More...

Some people believe the Money Pit is actually a sinkhole—a depression in the ground caused by water erosion.

WHAT Is the Mystery Behind Winchester House?

Staircases that lead nowhere, windows that look into other parts of the house, columns built upside-down. Those are just a few of the odd features visitors find when they tour the mysterious Winchester House in San Jose, California. Building started in 1884 and continued—uninterrupted—for the next 38 years. The construction ended only when the mansion's owner, Sarah Winchester, died. By that time, the mansion had 160 rooms, 361 steps, and 10,000 windowpanes.

Sarah was the widow of William Wirt Winchester, a wealthy rifle manufacturer. After her husband died in 1881, Sarah, who was very sad, visited a medium, someone who claimed to speak to the dead. The medium told Sarah she was haunted by the spirits of people killed by her husband's rifles. She wouldn't find peace unless Winchester built a home for herself but not complete it. According to the medium, an ever-changing house would confuse the ghosts. Sarah believed every word.

Today, Winchester House is on the National Register of Historic Places. If you are ever in San Jose, you can visit it and see it for yourself. Tour guides advise that you don't wander off. If you do, you might be lost for hours in the twisty maze of the building.

WHAT Were the Cottingley Fairies?

Do fairies really exist? According to Elsie Wright and her cousin Frances Griffiths, they do. And the two even took photos to prove it. In 1917, the girls claimed they saw fairies in the garden of Elsie's home in the English village of Cottingley. Elsie borrowed her father's camera and took a photograph of Frances with several of the spirits. A month later, Frances took a photo of Elsie shaking hands with a gnome.

The photos might have been forgotten, if Elsie's mother hadn't decided to show them to a man who believed the dead could talk to the living. He showed them to several people, including a photography expert who declared the pictures were genuine.

The Mystery Gets Solved

News of the photos spread. Then a famous writer asked the girls to take more pictures until there were a total of five.

Eventually the photos and the fairies were forgotten. It wasn't until the 1980s that Elsie admitted that she and her cousin had faked the pictures. She had drawn cutout figures of the fairies based on drawings from a children's book. Frances agreed that the first four photos were a hoax, but said that the fifth photo was real. Both women insisted that they had seen real live fairies.

Frances and the spirits. Real or fake?

Elsie shakes hands with a gnome.

WHAT Is a Rube Goldberg Machine?

Rube Goldberg machines—or contraptions—are designed to perform simple tasks in the most complicated, ridiculous, and hilarious way possible. Today, any needlessly complicated machine is called a Rube Goldberg, after its inventor, the cartoonist Reuben Goldberg.

The machines often begin with a simple action that sets off a chain reaction, as shown in these cartoons.

Reuben Lucius Goldberg (1883-1979), was an award-winning political cartoonist. Although Goldberg drew several cartoon series, he became most famous for Professor Lucifer Gorgonzola Butts. Butts was the cartoon inventor of such machines as one that showed how to remove cotton from a bottle of aspirin. Goldberg spent hours designing each machine to make sure that it would actually work. Even though Goldberg drew the zany machines, he never built one.

WHAT'S More . . .

The 1931 Merriam-Webster dictionary included the term "Rube Goldberg" as an adjective. The meaning: "Accomplishing by complex means what seemingly could be done simply."

How to Cut Your Own Hair

LAUGHING HYENA (A) LAUGHS- BLIND MOUSE(B) THINKS HYENA IS LAUGHING AT HIM, GETS INSULTED, WALKS OFF AND BUMPS INTO DISC(C) MOTION OF DISC IS TRANS-FERRED THROUGH SERIES OF RODS AND DISCS (D-E) TO STUFFED GLOVE (F), WHICH PUSHES WEAK, STARVING LILLIPUTIAN GOAT (G) AGAINST HEAD (H)- GOAT MOVES FORWARD AND EATS OFF HAIR UNTIL HE FALLS OVER INTO GOAT CRADLE(I)ON OTHER SIDE WHEN HE IS FULL.

N. B. ONE ORDINARY HEAD OF HAIR IS JUST ENOUGH TO FILL A REGULATION LILLIPUTIAN GOAT.

Automatic Sheet Music Turner

AT LAST! THE GREAT BRAIN OF THE DISTINGUISHED MAN OF SCIENCE GIVES THE WORLD THE SIMPLE AUTOMATIC SHEET MUSIC TURNER !

PRESS LEFT FOOT(A) ON PEDAL (B) WHICH PULLS DOWN HANDLE(C) ON TIRE PUMP (D). PRESSURE OF AIR BLOWS WHISTLE(E). GOLD FISH(F) BELIEVES THIS IS DINNER SIGNAL AND STARTS FEEDING ON WORM (G). THE PULL ON STRING (H) RELEASES BRACE(I), DROPPING SHELF (J), LEAVING WEIGHT (K) WITHOUT SUPPORT. NATURALLY, HATRACK (L) IS SUDDENLY EXTENDED AND BOXING GLOVE (M) HITS PUNCHING BAG(N) WHICH, IN TURN, IS PUNCTURED BY SPIKE (O).
ESCAPING AIR BLOWS AGAINST SAIL (P) WHICH IS ATTACHED TO PAGE OF MUSIC (Q), WHICH TURNS GENTLY AND MAKES WAY FOR THE NEXT OUTBURST OF SWEET OR SOUR MELODY.

Inventions change the way we live. It's hard to imagine our world without earmuffs or the ice-cream cone. In this chapter, you'll discover the amazing stories behind these inventions—and more!

How Zany Can You Get?

Many schools hold contests for students who want to design Rube Goldberg machines. One of the best known is a national event for college students held each year at Purdue University in Indiana. All contestants are assigned a specific task, such as "Sharpen a Pencil," "Shut Off an Alarm Clock," or "Water a Plant." Each machine is judged on how it performs, the number of steps needed to complete the task, and how well it keeps to the spirit of a Rube Goldberg machine.

Winners of the 2011 local Rube Goldberg competition at Purdue University

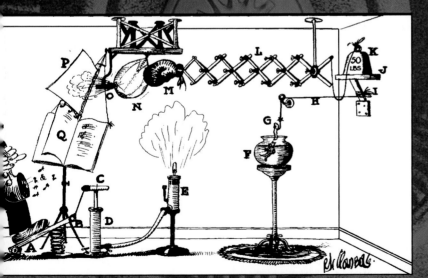

WHAT Is a Daguerreotype?

Click! Today, a digital camera can capture a scene in less than a second. That was not always so. In the early days of photography, it took up to 20 minutes to take a picture. These early photographs, called daguerreotypes (dah-*gehr*-oh-types), were produced by a process developed by Louis Daguerre who lived in France.

To take a daguerreotype, a photographer placed a silver-plated copper sheet covered with iodine into a camera and exposed it to light. Because the material wasn't very sensitive to light, it had to be exposed for a long time. Then the photographer placed the sheet in a cabinet with mercury vapor to develop the image. The fumes from the vapor combined with the silver to produce an image. To stop the developing process, the photographer rinsed the sheet in a salty solution.

Daguerreotypes caught on as more and more people wanted their picture taken. For the first time in history, people could preserve actual images of themselves and their loved ones. Unfortunately, daguerreotypes were very delicate and many of these early photographs faded or fell apart over time. By the 1850s, the daguerreotype became less popular as faster and cheaper ways to take photos became available.

Silver-plated sheet

Lens

Lens cap

Camera

WHAT'S More...

Posing for a daguerreotype portrait was time consuming. The process could take as long as 20 minutes. In order to not blur the photo, the person posing couldn't move.

In 1826, Joseph Niepce, a Frenchman who worked with Daguerre, took the world's first photograph. The photo needed an exposure time of eight hours. It shows a view of a city from a window.

The first photograph taken by Daguerre in 1837, shows plaster casts next to a window.

This 1847 daguerreotype shows French police making an arrest. It is thought to be the first news photo ever.

WHAT Is Djedi?

For hundreds of years, explorers have searched for secret passageways and concealed rooms inside the Great Pyramid of Giza, in Egypt. Now, a robot is finding what no explorer could. The robot, called Djedi, is part of a project led by an international team of researchers.

One of the pyramid's mysteries is what lies in the passageways beyond two eight-inch-square shafts. Because the narrow tunnels climb so high—they are equal to a 13-story building—only a robot can explore the entire length of the tunnel.

In 1993, a different robot reached the end of one of the passageways. But when it drilled through a wall, its camera revealed another wall. Djedi's advanced tools give it greater access, allowing it to explore further.

New Clues to Decode

One of the new robot's features is a snakelike camera, able to fit through small spaces and bend around corners. When Djedi got to the end of a passageway, it pushed its camera through a hole and peeked around the corner. There, it found red hieroglyphs and lines in the stone. The markings were last seen when the pyramid was built, more than 4,500 years ago.

Researchers believe that if the hieroglyphs can be deciphered, they may explain why the tunnels were built. What other secrets are hiding beyond a long shaft or behind a stone door? Perhaps a small robot will reveal the answers.

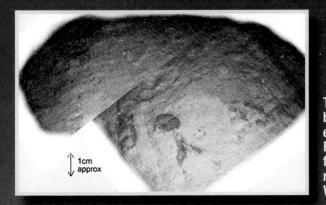

1cm
approx

The Djedi robot, below, has been exploring the Great Pyramid. The robot found the red markings at left. What do they mean?

The Great Pyramid at Giza is the largest of Egypt's 70 pyramids. When it was built around 2550 B.C., it was about 480 feet high.

WHAT Is a Penny Farthing Bicycle?

The old-fashioned penny farthing bicycle isn't seen much today, but during the 1870s and 1880s it was a common sight on cobblestone streets. With its extra-large front wheel, tiny back wheel, and tall seat, the penny farthing wasn't the easiest bike to ride. A rider needed a special mount just to climb onto the seat. Stopping the bike was also difficult because a rider couldn't put his foot on the ground. More importantly, the bike's high center of gravity made the bike unstable. Any obstacle, no matter how small, might tip the bike and send its rider flying.

This risk, however, didn't stop the penny farthing from becoming popular. That's because, unlike previous riding contraptions whose wheels were made of wood, the penny farthing had rubber tires, which gave people a much smoother ride. The large front wheel was directly connected to the pedals, which allowed a rider to go faster than ever before.

WHAT'S More...

How did the penny farthing bike get its name? In England, a farthing is a small coin, especially when compared to the much larger English penny. When the two coins are placed side-by-side, they look like the wheels of the high-wheeler bike.

Pedaling the Globe

The first person to circle the world by bike rode a penny farthing. Thomas Stevens set off from San Francisco on April 22, 1884. In his handlebar bag were clothes, a pistol, and a raincoat that doubled as his tent. Stevens rode across the United States along wagon trails, rail tracks, and paved roads. In some areas, he took trains.

When Stevens reached Boston, he sailed to Europe, where he resumed riding. He traveled through the continent to Asia.

Stevens' bike-riding journey ended on December 17, 1886, in Japan. From there he took a ship back to San Francisco. All together he had pedaled 13,500 miles. Stevens later wrote a book about his adventures, titled *Around the World on a Bicycle*.

WHAT Is GPS?

Before maps or compasses were invented, people used the sun and stars to navigate. In a way, we're still looking to the sky when we travel—only now we're looking to high-tech satellites, called the Global Positioning System (GPS).

GPS is a system of satellites, monitoring stations, and receivers. The 28 solar-powered satellites are spaced evenly around Earth and orbit our planet twice a day. Each satellite carries four atomic clocks that send the exact time to receivers on Earth. Each satellite also sends signals that tell its current location. A GPS receiver uses the information to calculate its own position on Earth.

Monitoring Stations

With so many satellites in orbit, it's important to know where each one is located to make sure none stray off course. Monitoring stations set up around the world do just that. The tracking information that the stations receive is relayed to the Master Control Station located at Schriever Air Force Base in Colorado.

Satellites in space send signals to monitoring stations on Earth.

WHAT'S More...

The United States developed GPS technology for military use. The public was allowed to use the system in 1983, although at first the information wasn't as precise as the military's.

Where Am I?

GPS has many uses on land, sea, and in the air. Besides helping drivers and pilots find their way, GPS keeps hikers on the right trail, and helps fishermen locate where the fish are biting. Golfers use it to measure the distance between holes.

Scientists use GPS to help them with their research, such as studying earthquake faults or discovering the migration patterns of animals. Explorers hunting for shipwrecks guide their vessels with GPS. And, perhaps most importantly, emergency teams responding to disasters use GPS to locate victims.

A motorcyclist checks his GPS to find the nearest road in Africa's Kalahari Desert.

Safe inside his truck, storm chaser Tim Samaras keeps an eye on an approaching tornado with the help of his GPS.

A hiker uses a map and GPS to plan her route up a mountain.

WHAT Are Some Inventions by Kids?

Inventors are a curious bunch, and many started tinkering and experimenting when they were kids. Here's a look at four inventions still in use today. What do they have in common? All were thought up by young inventors!

WHO: Margaret Knight, age 12
WHAT: Stop-motion safety device
WHEN: 1850
WHERE: New Hampshire

Margaret Knight's brothers worked in a cotton textile mill. One day, their younger sister paid them a visit, and while there, she witnessed a serious accident. A heavy machine malfunctioned and injured a worker. Knight went home and started tinkering. She invented a device that would automatically shut down a machine whenever a malfunction occurred. Knight went on to create many more inventions, including her most famous—a machine that folds and glues paper into bags with flat bottoms that's still in use today.

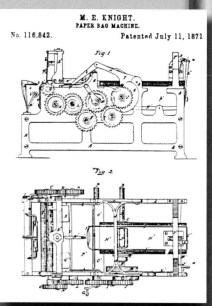

M. E. KNIGHT.
PAPER BAG MACHINE.
No. 116,842.   Patented July 11, 1871.
Fig 1
Fig 2

WHO: Louis Braille, age 15
WHAT: Braille
WHEN: 1924
WHERE: Paris, France

When he was three years old, Louis Braille became blind as a result of an infection. Braille went to school and memorized everything his teachers said. When he was 10, he entered a special school for the blind. Two years later, he heard a lecture about sonography, a method of reading and writing raised symbols that soldiers used so they could communicate at night.

When Braille was 15, he began fiddling with the "night writing," until he had a six-dot code. At age 20, he published an account that explained his code and how it worked. Braille's alphabet is now used in nearly every country in the world.

WHO: George Nissen, age 16
WHAT: Trampoline
WHEN: 1926 to 1934
WHERE: Cedar Rapids, Iowa

The circus had come to town, and George Nissen was staring at the trapeze artists as they glided through the air. As a gymnast on his high school's team, he must have watched in awe. He also noticed the netting that allowed the trapeze artists to bounce onto the swinging bars and caught them if they fell.

Nissen went home and started tinkering in his parents' garage. Before long, he devised a steel frame that he'd stretched with canvas. That early model was the beginning of what would become Nissen's great invention: the trampoline.

WHO: Chester Greenwood, age 15
WHAT: Earmuffs
WHEN: 1873
WHERE: Farmington, Maine

Except for the cold, Chester Greenwood enjoyed ice skating. Testing a new pair of skates on one especially freezing day, he couldn't keep his ears warm. Allergic to wool, he couldn't wear the scarves most kids used.

Frustrated, Greenwood took some wire and twisted it into two ovals. Then he asked his grandmother to sew fur onto them. That did the trick. Later, Greenwood fine-tuned his model and added a steel band to hold the muffs in place. He patented his invention, calling it the Greenwood's Champion Ear Protector. Today, we know them as earmuffs.

WHAT Are Some Foods Invented by Accident?

Many discoveries come about by accident or by an out-and-out mistake. When that happens with food inventions, the results are often lip-smackingly good.

WHAT: Chocolate Chip Cookies
WHO: Ruth Wakefield, innkeeper
WHEN: 1930
WHERE: Toll House Inn, Whitman, Massachusetts

One day, Ruth Wakefield ran out of baking chocolate while preparing a batch of cookies for her guests. All she had on hand was a chocolate candy bar, so she broke it up and added the pieces to her batter. She expected the chocolate to melt evenly. Instead, the cookies were studded with gooey bits of chocolate, and a new treat was born.

WHAT: Cereal Flakes
WHO: John Harvey Kellogg and Will Keith Kellogg
WHEN: 1894
WHERE: Battle Creek, Michigan

Waste not; want not. That's what the Kellogg brothers, who ran a home for people in poor health, believed. So when Will left some boiled wheat sitting out and it went stale, the two men attempted to turn it into long sheets of dough. Instead, the wheat came out of the rollers in flakes, which the brothers toasted and served to their patients. The cereal was a hit. Later, the brothers tried their new technique on other grains, including corn.

WHAT: Potato Chips
WHO: George Crum
WHEN: 1853
WHERE: Moon Lake House, Saratoga Springs, New York

Customers can be tough to please. Chef George Crum knew that all too well. A guest at his inn kept returning his fried potatoes, claiming they weren't crisp enough. The chef had enough. He sliced a new batch of potatoes as thin as he could, fried them in oil, and sprinkled salt on them. The dish wasn't returned and soon other guests wanted their potatoes made the same way.

WHAT: Ice-Cream Cones
WHO: Ernest Hamwi
WHEN: 1904
WHERE: World's Fair, St. Louis, Missouri

Arnold Fornachou, a vendor at the fair, had just run out of paper dishes to serve his ice cream, and customers were lining up. He turned to his fellow vendors for help. Ernest Hamwi came to the rescue. He rolled up his waffle-like pastries and gave them to Fornachou to fill with ice cream. Later, Hamwi received a patent for a pastry cone-making machine and started his own company.

WHAT Is a Dirigible?

Any aircraft that's filled with a lighter-than-air gas and can be steered is a dirigible. Instead of wings like an airplane, a dirigible uses rudders and propellers to navigate through the air. There are two basic kinds of dirigibles. One is the rigid airship, which has a rigid frame, or skeleton, underneath its covering. The second kind is the blimp, which doesn't have a rigid frame. Both types are filled with helium—a gas that enables the dirigibles to fly.

Henri Giffard flew the first prototype of the dirigible in the 1850s. By the early 1900s, they were popular across the world. Today, dirigibles are mostly used for advertising and sightseeing purposes. If you go to pro-football games, you may have seen a blimp providing overhead coverage of the game.

A blimp doesn't have a rigid frame, so it deflates like a balloon when its helium is removed.

The *Hindenburg* Disaster

The *Hindenburg*, a luxury airship built by Zeppelin, a German company, was the largest airship in the world. More than 800 feet long, it needed more than 7 million cubic feet of hydrogen to fill it. On May 3, 1937, it took off from Frankfurt, Germany. Aboard were 61 crew members and 36 passengers. Three days later, it attempted to land at Lakehurst, New Jersey, in poor weather conditions. Suddenly the airship caught fire and was consumed in flames. Remarkably, 62 of the people on board survived. To this day, no one knows for sure what started the fire, but because the airship used flammable hydrogen instead of the safer helium, it burned in minutes.

WHAT Is Kevlar?

Plenty of police officers and soldiers owe their lives to Kevlar, the main material used in bullet-proof vests. Considered a miracle fiber, Kevlar has five times the strength of steel yet is lightweight and flexible. Another big plus is that it doesn't rust, corrode, or tear. That makes it an ideal material to use in underwater cables, boat hulls, and pieces of spacecraft.

A New Spin on Fiber

So how did such a super-strong fiber come about? In 1964, Stephanie Kwolek was working as a researcher for DuPont, an American chemical company. Her team was asked to develop high-performance fibers that were strong, lightweight, and that didn't melt at high temperatures.

One day she melted a polymer—a substance that nylon, rubber, and vinyl are made of—into a liquid. Kwolek took the solution to be spun in a spinneret, a machine that turns liquid polymers into fiber. The fiber that came out was tested to see how strong it was. The results were amazing. The fiber was both strong and lightweight. Today, Kevlar is used to make safety helmets, firefighters' suits, radial tires, suspension bridge cables, brake pads, and racing sails.

WHAT'S More . . .

Ounce for ounce, Kevlar is stronger than steel, but spider silk is even stronger. And toughest of all is the silk from the Darwin's bark spider, an arachnid that lives in the jungles of Madagascar. The orb webs from these spiders are enormous, and can span rivers, streams, and lakes.

WHAT Is a Boomerang?

The boomerang is a curved missile that spins through the air and may return to the thrower. Boomerangs have been around for a very long time. One discovered in Poland, was carved from a mammoth's tusk and is about 30,000 years old. Experts say it was a non-returning boomerang—it didn't come back after it was thrown. They think it was used as a weapon to hunt animals.

Returning boomerangs were first used in Australia about 10,000 years ago. There, the native people, called Aborigines, developed a returning boomerang for fun and sport. And that's the role they still play today.

Modern boomerangs can be shaped like a banana, an *X*, or a question mark. Today's versions are made from a variety of materials, including plywood, plastic, aluminum, and fiberglass.

WHAT'S More...

Boomerang fans test their skills at tournaments. They compete at different events, such as long distance, doubling (throwing two boomerangs at the same time), and fast catch (the most catches in five minutes).

A player competes in a boomerang championship in Delaware.

A Really **BIG** Boomerang

At almost 9 feet from tip to tip and weighing 2.3 pounds, the world's largest returning boomerang is not easy to throw. The boomerang has a handle where its two wings meet. The thrower holds the handle and hoists the boomerang on his back before launching it forward. It can fly about 75 feet.

Make Your Own Boomerang

What You Need

- cardboard from the back of an old cereal box
- ruler
- pencil
- scissors
- stapler

What to Do

1. Measure and cut out two 8-inch x 3/4-inch rectangles from the cardboard.

2. Place one rectangle over the other so that the two pieces are perpendicular to each other. Staple through the center where they cross. You should now have an X-shaped object with four arms.

3. Cut 1/8 inch off the side of each arm as shown.

4. Round each arm's tip.

5. To throw your boomerang, go outdoors. Holding one of the arms vertically at its tip, bring the boomerang so that it is just past your ear.

6. Then move your forearm forward, flicking your wrist as you do so and releasing the boomerang. If you don't get your boomerang to return on the first try, keep practicing until you get the hang of it.

WHAT Is a Geodesic Dome?

A geodesic dome is hard to miss. The structure is shaped like a partial sphere and it's made up of interlocking pyramid shapes called tetrahedrons. Lightweight, yet extremely strong and stable, the geodesic dome uses less material to cover more space than any other structure ever built.

A Man Ahead of His Time

The man who patented the geodesic dome was Buckminster Fuller, an American engineer and inventor. In the 1950s, he designed the geodesic dome in an effort to provide low-cost housing. While the domes never caught on as places to live, they are used as airplane hangars, greenhouses, observatories, theaters, sports arenas, and planetariums.

Buckminster Fuller stands in front of one of his geodesic domes.

WHAT'S More...

Before Fuller's invention, domes needed to be supported with vaults or flying buttresses.

flying buttress

vault

Famous Geodesic Domes

Designed by Buckminster Fuller for Expo 67, the 1967 world's fair in Montreal, Canada, the Biosphere is now a museum dedicated to the environment.

A complete sphere, Spaceship Earth is more a globe than a dome. Still, the Disney World attraction is perhaps the most famous geodesic dome ever built. It towers 180 feet high and can easily be seen for miles around.

Located in Toronto, Canada, the SkyDome, home to the Toronto Blue Jays, is a geodesic dome with a retractable roof. On sunny days, the roof can open completely so players and fans can enjoy the weather. When it rains or snows, the roof closes.

WHAT Is a Hovercraft?

Imagine a vehicle that can travel on water, land, or ice. Does that make it a plane, a car, or a boat? It's the hovercraft, a vehicle that glides over land or sea on a cushion of air powered by air propellers or jet engines.

High-pressurized vents of air supplied by a powered fan underneath the craft press down on the surface, lifting the vehicle slightly. This constant air source is trapped by the vehicle's skirt, reducing friction and allowing it to move forward smoothly.

A Crafty Inventor

Christopher Cockerell, an English inventor, wanted to make the boat he was building go faster. He figured that a vehicle suspended on a cushion of air would quickly skim the water's surface. However, any fan he used would be larger than the boat. After trial and error, Cockerell realized that pressurized air around the rim of the boat could cause it to rise.

Out of Luck, Then Success

In 1952, Cockerell got busy designing and testing a model. He took it to the British government, thinking the armed forces could benefit from his invention. Although his idea was classified top secret, Cockerell didn't receive any money to develop the hovercraft further. He later complained, "The Navy said it was a plane not a boat; the Air Force said it was a boat not a plane; and the Army were 'plain not interested.'"

Five years later, the inventor built a full-scale model, the SR-N1. On July 25, 1959, the SR-N1 successfully crossed the English Channel in a little over two hours.

The SR-N1

This hovercraft is about to come ashore on a beach in Japan.

What Are They Good For?

Hovercraft transport people, equipment, and other vehicles across all kinds of terrain.

O Hovercraft fly over shallow water, thin ice, rapids, swamps, and even deserts to rescue people in danger.

O The military uses hovercraft to transport tanks and other heavy equipment.

O Oil companies use flat-deck hovercraft to transport equipment across mud flats.

CHAPTER ⑫ The Future

WHAT Will Future Transportation Be Like?

Cars

Many transportation innovations of the future already exist. The challenge is how to make these energy-saving vehicles work more efficiently so they can replace the fossil-fuel vehicles we ride in today. For instance, electric vehicles that run on batteries need to be improved so they can travel longer distances. Today, an electric car can run for about 100 miles before its battery has to be recharged.

Engineers are developing an electric two-wheeled vehicle called P.U.M.A. (Personal Urban Mobility and Accessibility). Running on a lithium battery, the small, space-saving, 300-pound vehicle would ease city traffic jams.

What will the future hold? Will we go to work in flying cars? Vacation on the moon? Snarf down meat grown in test tubes? Here are some expert predictions.

Trains

Today, commuters in some big cities in China and Japan ride on high-speed maglev trains. (Maglev stands for magnetic levitation.) Such a train doesn't need wheels. Instead, it uses magnets to raise—or levitate—the train inches above the track. Futurists—people who think about the future and how we will live—believe maglevs will replace traditional trains in the U.S and around the world.

A maglev can travel at speeds of more than 300 mph, offering smooth, quiet rides.

Planes

Other solutions for future transportation exist only as ideas. Personal flying vehicles are an exciting possibility. A NASA engineer designed the Puffin, a one-person, electric, flying craft. Right now the Puffin is just a concept, but one day you might zip around in one.

To fly the Puffin, the pilot lies flat on his or her stomach. When not in use, the vehicle would rest on its tail.

WHAT Will Space Travel Be Like?

Sixty years ago, space travel existed only in science-fiction novels. Today, astronauts have landed on the moon and lived in space for more than a year. What will the future hold for travel to the farthest reaches of our solar system?

Solar Sail

A spacecraft's weight is about 95 percent rocket fuel, making long-distance space flight extremely expensive. But what if there were a way to reduce the amount of fuel by harnessing the sun's energy to propel spacecraft once they reach space? Engineers are experimenting with solar-sail powered craft. Such a craft, made of lightweight, reflective material, would use sunlight as its power. Light particles bouncing off the reflective sail would push the craft forward at a faster and faster speed. A solar sail, however, would not be able to reach space on its own. It would need a traditional rocket to launch it. Once in space, though, the sail would have endless power from the sun and could travel indefinitely.

People
money
spare c
go on a
week-lo
visit to
Interna
Space S

Space Tourism

Do you have 20 million dollars to spare? That's the current price for a one-week stay at the International Space Station. So far, at least five people have paid to experience life in space. Like astronauts, the tourists must prepare for their trip, spending several months training. In the years to come, more and more people will visit space. There is even talk of developing space hotels, where tourists could vacation and take spacewalks.

Elevator to the Stars

Engineers are developing an elevator to send people into space without rockets! The space elevator would let a spacecraft climb a cable into the sky. Made of a paper-thin yet incredibly strong and flexible material, a ribbon-shaped cable would reach more than 60,000 miles into space where it would end at a platform. The bottom of the cable would be anchored in the ocean. People and cargo would ride up the elevator on mechanical lifters. Once at the top, they would board a traditional spacecraft and zoom off to their final destination.

Platfo

EART

WHAT Will We Be Eating for Dinner?

In the next 50 years, another two to three billion people will be living—and eating—on Earth. With so many mouths to feed, scientists are looking for ways to guarantee there will be enough food to go around. This may include developing super crops that resist disease, insects, and weather extremes, so that they yield bigger harvests. Eating readily available sources of protein, such as insects and algae, simple, one-celled plants, is another suggestion.

But probably the most unusual idea of what will be on our table years from now is meat grown in laboratories. Why would scientists want to do that? Raising livestock takes up a lot of land. The animals consume huge amounts of plants and put out greenhouse gases that are bad for the environment.

When cows belch and pass gas, they give off methane, a greenhouse gas that traps heat in the atmosphere and has been linked to global warming. One adult cow can produce up to 400 pounds a year. Worldwide, cows and other cud-chewing animals produce 80 million metric tons of the gas.

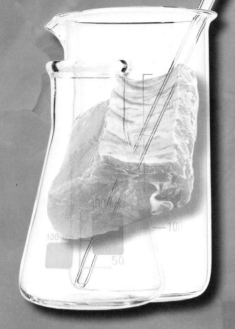

The first meat successfully grown in a lab came from goldfish cells. NASA conducted the experiments in 2000, hoping to provide astronauts on long space trips with fresh meat. Nine years later, Dutch scientists produced pork from the cells of a pig.

Although it is technically possible to make test-tube meat, scientists are not able to produce it in large amounts. Plus it takes about one million dollars to produce 8 ounces of test-tube beef. (That's one pricey steak!) Until scientists figure out how to make it cheaper and quicker, test-tube meat will only be food for thought.

Dirt-Free Salad

Carrots, radishes, and lettuce grown without soil? In the future, that might be how most vegetables are raised. It's all thanks to hydroponics—a way to grow crops in water without a speck of soil. As Earth's population skyrockets and farming land declines, hydroponics will provide farmers with another choice. Crops can thrive in underground vaults, on rooftops, greenhouses, and in buildings designed for this space-saving farming method.

WHAT Animals May Become Extinct?

More than 230 million years ago, dinosaurs walked the planet. About 165 million years later, they were extinct, most likely done in by a massive asteroid that crashed into Earth.

In the not-so-distant future, many species of animals that are alive today may follow in the dinosaurs' footsteps. Most will have been done in not by an object from space, but because of humans. As people chop down more and more forests, take over vast amounts of land for crops, and pollute the air and oceans, animals are disappearing at a frightening rate.

Top 10 Endangered Species

Leatherback turtle

Sumatran orangutan

Mountain gorilla

Atlantic bluefin tuna

Vaquita

Source: World Wildlife Fund

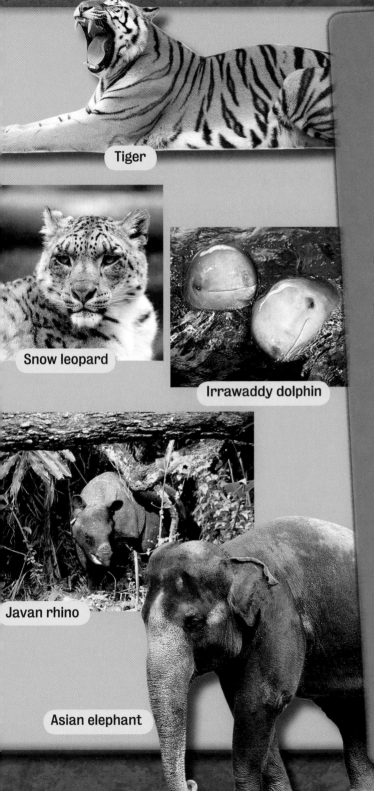

Tiger

Snow leopard

Irrawaddy dolphin

Javan rhino

Asian elephant

Your Help Matters

The good news is that conservation efforts have helped save many animals from becoming extinct. In the 1960s, the bald eagle was in danger of being wiped out, with fewer than 450 nesting pairs in the continental U.S. Today, there are close to 10,000 couples and the future looks bright.

Here are some ways you can help save threatened animals.

- Learn all you can about endangered animals. The more you know, the more you can help.

- Share what you learn with others. Pick an endangered animal and do a school project on it, or design a poster and put it up where people can see it.

- Write and put on a play about an endangered animal. Cast your friends and perform it at school or at a community center.

- Hold a fundraiser for endangered animals. You and your friends and neighbors can raise money by holding a bake sale, a car wash, or a yard sale.

- Adopt an endangered animal. Many organizations allow you to "adopt" an animal. The World Wildlife Fund is a good place to start.

- Volunteer at a nature center or wildlife refuge that cares for endangered animals.

- Write a letter to your senators or representative and tell them why it is important to protect endangered species. Encourage your friends and neighbors to write, too.

Glossary

acid rain precipitation that has high acidity because of being mixed with pollutants

air pressure the weight of the atmosphere that pushes down on people and objects

algae primitive plants that have no roots, stems, or leaves, and live mainly in water

alkaline having a pH level above seven; the opposite of acidic

amphibian a cold-blooded animal with a backbone, such as a frog, that is born in water and then lives on land when adult

anemometer an instrument used to measure wind speed

Antarctica the ice-covered continent around the South Pole

aquatic living or growing in water

arachnid an arthropod having four pairs of legs, such as spiders and scorpions

archaeologist a scientist who studies how people in the past lived using information gained from artifacts of that culture, such as pottery and tools

Arctic the area around the North Pole

arthropod invertebrates (animals without backbones) with hard, segmented bodies and jointed legs, such as insects and shrimp

asteroid rocks, some the size of small planets, that orbit between Mars and Jupiter

atmosphere the envelope of gases around the Earth

axon the part of a nerve cell that carries impulses away from the body of a cell

bacteria microscopic, single-celled organisms found in water, air, and soil

botanist a scientist who studies plants

camanchaca heavy fog that forms in the Atacama Desert and moves inland

carapace a hard covering on the back of certain animals, such as turtles

carnivore an animal that primarily eats meat

cartilage a tough, flexible type of connective tissue

cells the basic structure of all living things

cerebral cortex the wrinkled outer layer of gray matter in the brain; the part of the brain mainly used in learning

chicle a gummy substance from tropical trees that is used to make chewing gum

climate weather conditions in one place over a long period of time

collagen a fibrous type of protein that connects and supports tissues in the body, such as skin, tendons, and muscles

colloid a mixture in which tiny particles of one substance are dispersed through a second substance

coma a thin cloud that surrounds a comet, made up from its heated gases and dust; a comet's coma can extend for millions of miles

comet a large chunk of rock surrounded by frozen gas and ice that orbits the sun

compound eye an eye made up of several simple eyes; most insects have compound eyes

dark energy a form of energy that astronomers believe is responsible for the universe expanding at an increasing rate

dark matter an invisible form of matter that astronomers believe affects gravitational forces in the universe

dendrite a nerve cell that carries impulses to the body of a cell

dirigible an aircraft that can be steered or guided

double-jointed having unusually flexible joints that can bend more than most people's

dust devil a small whirlwind that raises a column of dust and debris

dyslexia a learning disability in which a person has difficulty recognizing and understanding written words

echidna an egg-laying mammal of Australia and surrounding regions that has a long snout and a spiny coat

electron a tiny particle that moves around the nucleus of an atom

endangered a species, or type of living thing, that is in immediate danger of becoming extinct, or dying out completely

flying buttress a support built against a wall and forming an arch

fossil part of a plant or animal from the distant past that has been preserved in the Earth's crust

fossil fuels fuels, such as oil and coal, that are created by plant and animal matter over millions of years

gland a cell or group of cells that produces a substance that a body uses or gets rid of

global warming an increase in the average temperature of the Earth

GPS (Global Positioning System) a satellite navigation system that is used to determine an exact location on Earth

gravity the force of attraction between two objects

greenhouse gas a gas, such as carbon dioxide or methane, that helps cause global warming

grub wormlike larva of certain insects, such as beetles

herbivore an animal that feeds on plants

hieroglyphic a type of writing, such as one used by ancient Egyptians, that uses picture symbols to represent words or sounds

Hopi a Native American tribe, most living in northeastern Arizona

hydroponics a method of growing plants in nutrient solutions rather than soil

hypergiant a star even more massive than a supergiant, hypergiant has a diameter that is 100 to 2,100 times the size of the sun's, and is extremely bright

immigrant a person who moves permanently to another country from his or her native land

immune system cells, proteins, and tissue that protect the body from infection and disease

invertebrate an animal that does not have a backbone

Jacobson's Organ one of two sacs in the roof of the mouth that certain animals, such as snakes, use to locate smells

jazz a type of music with African-American roots developed in the 20th century and characterized by improvisation and intricate rhythms

joint the part of the body where two bones are connected

kachina one of hundreds of spiritual beings that play an important part in Hopi religious practices

kiva an underground room used for religious rituals by members of southwestern Native American tribes, such as the Hopi

kookaburra an Australian bird with a loud, harsh cry

larva the earliest stage of an animal, just after it has hatched and before it changes into an adult

larynx in people, the part of the throat that contains vocal cords

living fossil an animal or plant that closely resembles species known from fossils

lunar eclipse an eclipse in which the moon passes through the umbra of the Earth's shadow

Madagascar an island off the southeastern coast of Africa

magnetic fields the lines of force surrounding the sun and the planets, generated by electrical currents

malaria an infectious disease transmitted by mosquitoes

mammal a warm-blooded vertebrate (having a backbone) that has hair or fur; mammals feed milk to their young.

mammalian diving reflex a reflex that allows mammals to stay underwater for long periods of time by slowing down the body's metabolism and compressing the lungs

marine biologist a scientist who studies ocean life

marsupial a warm-blooded vertebrate (having a backbone) that has an external pouch in which to carry and feed its young

mastodon an extinct elephant-like mammal that lived more than two million years ago

metabolism all the chemical processes that take place within a living organism that are necessary to sustain life

meteorite a mass of stone or metal that has fallen from space

meteorologist a scientist who studies the climate and weather

molecule the smallest part of a substance, made up of one or more atoms

mollusk an invertebrate (animal without a backbone) that usually has a shell that covers its soft body; snails and squid are mollusks

monotreme a type of mammal, such as the platypus, that lays eggs rather than gives birth to live young

monsoon a wind that changes direction with the seasons, especially the seasonal wind of India and southern Asia

musher a person who takes part in cross-country races with a dog team and sled

mycologist a scientist who studies fungi

myelin sheath a fatty wrapping found around certain nerve axons that speeds up neural impulses

narwhal a small whale that lives in the Arctic; the male has a long, twisted tusk

neuron a cell of the nervous system that consists of an axon and dendrites

nocturnal active at night

nutrient a substance that an organism needs to live and grow

omnivore an animal that eats both other animals and plants

orbit the path one body takes around another, such as the path of the Earth around the sun

penumbra the outer, partially lighted shadow that surrounds the complete shadow (umbra) of a heavenly body during an eclipse

pH a number that expresses whether a solution is an acid or a base; a pH of 7 is neutral

pheromones chemicals produced by an animal that affect the behavior of other animals

pod a small herd of animals, especially seals or whales

pollution the contamination of air, water, or soil by harmful substances

polymer a natural or synthetic compound that is made up of repeated links of simple molecules

precipitation rain, snow, or hail

predator an animal that hunts other animals for food

prehistoric related to a period of time before history was recorded

primate a mammal that has such features as a large brain, five digits on their hands and feet; monkeys, apes, and humans are primates

proboscis a long, flexible trunk or snout of certain animals, such as an elephant's

protein a substance basic to living cells and necessary for an organism to function; it is an important source of energy in a person's diet

proton a stable particle in the nucleus of an atom

radiation electromagnetic energy that moves in the form of waves

resin a sticky substance given off by fir trees; used to make plastics, medicines, and varnishes

satellite a natural or manmade object that revolves around a planet

solar eclipse an eclipse in which the sun is obscured by the moon

space probe an unmanned spacecraft designed to explore the solar system and send information back to Earth

species a group of similar organisms

spinneret a machine that turns liquid polymers into fiber

stockade a defensive barrier made of stakes or timber

stylet a thin, stiff, needlelike feeding organ that all true insects have

supergiant a star at least 100 times the sun's diameter and much brighter

supernova the explosion of a star

swim bladder an inflated sac found in most bony fish that helps them stay afloat

taxidermy the art of preserving dead animals by stuffing and mounting their skins

tendon a tissue connecting muscle to bone

territorial defending one's land or territory

tetrahedron a solid figure formed by four triangular faces

tornado a dark, funnel-shaped cloud made of fast-spinning air

tusk a long, constantly growing front tooth that appears, usually in pairs, in certain animals, such as elephants

ulnar nerve a nerve that runs along the inner side of the arm and passes close to the surface of the skin near the elbow; also known as the funny bone

umbra the darkest part of a shadow, cast by one heavenly body on another

vaccine a medicine made of dead or weakened germs that prevents a person from getting sick from that germ

vacuum a space completely free of matter or air

venom a poisonous substance produced by certain snakes and insects, usually given off in a bite or sting

Index

332 Fighter Group, 123

©redits

Endpapers: Noel Powell, Schaumburg/shutterstock
Back cover: David McNew/Getty Images (mask); Shebeko/shutterstock (ice-cream cone); David Haring/DUPC/Getty Images (aye-aye); Matt Anker/ Getty Images (anemometer); Jorg Hackemann/ shutterstock (zorbing)

p 2: Erik Lam/shutterstock (bloodhound); sunsetman/shutterstock (mudskipper); SSPL/Getty Images (orrery)

p 3: WireImage/Getty Images (contortionist); kzww/shutterstock (herring); Babk Tafreshi/Getty Images (eclipse); National Geographic/Getty Images (statue); Heidi Zech/Getty Images (ackee and hands)

p 4: Matt Jeppson/shutterstock (large snake); Sankei/ Getty Images (horse vault); Gary S. Chapman/Getty Images (passport); Harvey Lloyd/ Getty Images (kachina doll); Howard Kingsnorth/ Getty Images (GPS); Bob Carey for Segway Inc. (GM P.U.M.A)

pp 6-7: Andrew Kerr/shutterstock (dog's nose); Erik Lam/shutterstock (bloodhound)

pp 8-9: Dorling Kindersley/Getty Images (snake); Karl Ammann /Getty Images (zebra); Roy Toft/Getty Images (lion); Digital Vision/Getty Images (horse); Gallo Images-Heinrich van den Berg/Getty Images (elephant)

pp 10-11: David Haring/DUPC/Getty Images (aye-aye, center and bottom); Mark Carwardine/ Getty Images (hand); Minden Pictures (lemur)

pp 12-13: Talvi/shutterstock (African elephant); Richard Peterson/shutterstock (Asian elephant); Ben Cranke/Getty Images (trunk, p.12); Joel Sartore/ Getty Images (trunk, p.13)

pp 14-15: Michal Ninger/shutterstock (kookaburra); kzww/shutterstock (herring, top); Paul Nicklen/Getty Images (herring, bottom)

pp 16-17: Chungking/shutterstock (snakehead); National Geographic/Getty Images (catfish); sunsetman/shutterstock (mudskipper, top); Ivan Kuzmin/shutterstock (mudskipper, bottom); Joe McDonald/Getty Images (axolotl)

pp 18-19: Paul Nicklen/Getty Images (both photos)

pp 20-21: John Carnemolla/shutterstock (echidna); Dorling Kindersley/Getty Images (echidna illustration); Tom McHugh/Getty Images (platypus); De Agostini/Getty Images (platypus illustration)

pp 22-23: Henrik Larsson/shutterstock (main photo); Mike Dubose (family); almond/shutterstock (jellyfish); Oksana Potyomkina/shutterstock (hippo); Guy J. Sagi/shutterstock (deer)

pp 24-25: OlegD/shutterstock (horseshoe crab, left); Marcel Clemens/shutterstock (fossil); Marques/ shutterstock (main photo); Creative Commons (coelacanth); Vudhikrai/shutterstock (nautilus); Pongphan.R/shutterstock (cockroach)

pp 26-27: All photos by NASA, ESA, and R. Humphreys (University of Minnesota)

pp 28-29: NASA (Coma cluster); Stocktrek Images/ Getty Images (spiral galaxy); SSPL/Getty Images (man with telescope); NASA (Milky Way)

pp 30-31: All photos by NASA

pp 32-33: NASA/Newsmakers/Getty Images (Jupiter); Space Frontiers/Hulton Archive/Getty Images (Ganymede); NASA/SSPL/Getty Images (top comet); Datacraft Co Ltd/Getty Images (bottom comet); Dieter Spannknebel/Getty Images (asteroid and Earth); Dieter Spannknebel/Getty Images (Vesta asteroid)

pp 34-35: Public domain (painting); SSPL/Getty Images (large orrery); Nicholas Chatfield-Taylor courtesy of of The Long Now Foundation, www.longnow.org (Long Now orrery); Courtesy of Miruna D. Popescu (human orrery)

pp 36-37: Babk Tafreshi/Getty Images (eclipse); Stocktrek Images/Getty Images (diagram); Chung Sung-Jun/Getty Images (people with glasses)

pp 38-39: Lazar Mihai-Bogdan/shutterstock (moon); Mike Copeland/Getty Images (Hoba meteorite); Creative Commons (Cape York meteorite)

pp 40-41: Roberto Gonzalez/Getty Images (Endeavour); NASA/Bill Ingalls (Atlantis); NASA; timeline: NASA/Getty Images (2); ESA/NASA/ Getty Images

pp 42-43: All photos by NASA

pp 44-45: Creative Commons (neuron diagram); Anatomical Travelogue/Getty Images (brain)

pp 46-47: Roman Gorielov/shutterstock (book); agsandrew/shutterstock (music); bbbar/shutterstock (numbers); siamionau pavel/shutterstock (painting); Jaimie Duplass/shutterstock (girl with basketball); R studio T (head); Maksim Shmeljov/shutterstock (shaking hands); djgis/shutterstock (landscape)

pp 48-49: Mixa/Getty Images (kid with headphones); Will & Deni McIntyre/Getty Images (notebook); Jon Kopaloff/FilmMagic/Getty Images (Cruise); Jemal Countess/FilmMagic/Getty Images (Knightley); Focus on Sport/Getty Images (Ali); Robyn Beck/AFP/Getty Images (Spielberg)

pp 50-51: Vladimir Wrangel/shutterstock (girl eating corn); Creations/shutterstock (heart); Kati Neudert/shutterstock (eye); AISPIX by Image Source/shutterstock (tongue); Tinydevil/shutterstock (gluteus maximus); Sergieiev/shutterstock (sidebar); Sergieiev/shutterstock (arm)

pp 52-53: Bernd Schmidt/shutterstock (man); Pennyimages/shutterstock (apple); Alila Sao Mai/ shutterstock (diagram); Piotr Marcinski/ shutterstock (arm)

pp 54-55: PM Images/Getty Images (female contortionist); WireImage/Getty Images (male contortionist); Medical Images/Getty Images (joints); Falater Photography/shutterstock (gymnast); Goldmund Lukic/Getty Images (yogi); Biophoto Associates/Getty Images (hands)

pp 56-57: XuRa/shutterstock (Atacama Desert); John Warburton-Lee/Getty Images (plants in desert)

pp 58-59: Creative Commons (Aziziya); shutterstock (Death Valley); public domain (Russian research station); Antonov Roman/shutterstock (raindrops); nulinukas/shutterstock (snow)

pp 60-61: NASA (large photo); Arctic-Images/Getty Images (Iceland photo) Antony Spencer/Getty Images (trees); Stocktrek/Getty Images (aurora australis)

pp 62-63: ASIF HASSAN/AFP/Getty Images (Pakistan); John Henry Claude Wilson /Getty Images (India); India Today Group/Getty Images (crops)

pp 64-65: Oxford Scientific/Getty Images (dead trees); Dr. Marli Miller/Getty Images (obelisk); Will & Deni McIntyre/Getty Images (scientist in forest); National Geographic/Getty Images (statue, left); W. K. Fletcher/Getty Images (statue, right) National Geographic/Getty Images (salamander)

pp 66-67: Georg Rosen/Getty Images (Nordensklold); Sue Flood/Getty Images (icebreaker)

pp 68-69: Wood/Getty Images (dust devil); NASA (Martian dust devil)

pp 70-71: SSPL via Getty Images (anemometer, top); Matt Anker/Getty Images (anemometer, bottom); Ryan McGinnis/Getty Images (wind anemometer); Courtesy of Dantec Dynamics A/S (laser anemometer); Courtesy of R.M. Young Company (ultrasound anemometer)

pp 72-73: Piti Tan /shutterstock (main photo); Debu55y/shutterstock (asparagus); Valentyn Volkov/ shutterstock (coconut); Valery121283/shutterstock (eggplant); wavebreakmedia ltd./shutterstock (gavel); Yellowj/shutterstock (tomato)

pp 74-75: Kavee/shutterstock (beans); Pakhnyushcha/shutterstock (salmon); martiapunts/ shutterstock (pasta); eurobanks/shutterstock (olive oil); Evgeny Karandaev/shutterstock (milk); Fotofermer/shutterstock (carrots); gosphotodesign/ shutterstock (girl); Quang Ho/shutterstock (sweet potatoes); Teze/shutterstock (blueberries)

pp 76-77: Kbrowne4/shutterstock (shark); Dennis MacDonald/Getty Images (bear); WitthayaP/ shutterstock (zebra); Coaster/Alamy (cat); vanillaechoes/shutterstock (tofu salad)

pp 78-79: Nito/shutterstock (gummy candy); Dasha Petrenko /shutterstock (chocolate); Ildi Papp/ shutterstock (gelatin molds); White Packert/Getty Images (kid with shampoo); GLYPHstock/shutterstock (paintballs); 54613/shutterstock (dessert)

pp 80-81: Smithsonian National Air and Space Museum (meals x 3); AFP/Getty Images (Glenn); NASA/Getty Images (Young & Grissom)

pp 82-83: David Kirkland/Getty Images (witchetty grubs); Hoang Dinh Nam/AFP/Getty Images (crickets); Wojtek Jarco/shutterstock (stink bug); Nathan Dexter/AFP/Getty Images (tarantulas); D. Kucharski & K. Kucharska/shutterstock (worm)

pp 84-85: Heidi Zech/Getty Images (ackee and hands); Jan Halaska/Getty Images (tree); Rohit Seth/shutterstock (ackee and codfish); pixbox77/ shutterstock (cassava); Creative Commons (puffer fish); majaan/shutterstock (mushrooms)

pp 86-87: Julian Rovagnati/shutterstock (boy); Steliost /shutterstock (resin, top); SSPL/Getty Images (chicle jar); Royster/shutterstock (resin, bottom); Creative Commons (tar)

pp 88-89: David Boily/AFP/Getty Images (poutine); Jonelle Weaver/Getty Images (borscht); Dan Goldberg/Getty Images (adobo); Paul Cowan/ shutterstock (haggis); Chung Sung-Jun/Getty Images (kimchi)

pp 90-91: Nagel Photography/shutterstock (black bear, bottom); lightpoet/shutterstock (bear, open mouth); Tony Campbell/shutterstock (bear, standing); Matt Jeppson/shutterstock (large snake); Casey K. Bishop/shutterstock (rattlesnake); Ryan M. Bolton/shutterstock (cottonmouth); Matt Jeppson/ shutterstock (coral snake & sidewinder)

What Are Nutrients?

What Is a Dust Devil?

What Is a Narwhal?

WHAT Will Future Transportation Be Like?

What If You Run into a Bear in the Wild?

WHAT Is Mancala?

What Are Some Foods Invented by Accident?

What Is Tanabata?